W9-AQI-737

Complete Guide to
EXPLORATORY FOREIGN LANGUAGE PROGRAMS

Dora F. Kennedy
Prince George's County
Public Schools, Maryland

William E. De Lorenzo
University of Maryland

NATIONAL TEXTBOOK COMPANY • Lincolnwood, Illinois U.S.A.

This work is dedicated to all subject areas which comprise the interdisciplinary content of the exploratory curriculum as presented in this book.

And, to all those in the foreign language profession who are, have been, and will be involved in the development and implementation of Exploratory courses throughout the country.

Contents

Chapter 5

Preparation of the Exploratory Teacher

Chapter 6

Representative Materials and Resources

Chapter 7

Observations and Future Considerations

Foreword

Most foreign language educators have hailed the assessments of education that have emerged from such groups as the National Commission on Excellence in Education, the College Board, the Twentieth Century Fund, and the Carnegie Corporation, for these assessments have, for the most part, called for increased second-language study from kindergarten through high school. These assessments, however, pose a challenge to foreign language teachers; they do not necessarily call for academic achievement but rather the attainment of fluency or proficiency.

Because students must be prepared for extended sequences of study if they are to attain fluency or proficiency, foreign language educators must give careful attention to two critical needs of all potential foreign language students: a readiness for second-language learning and a sound basis for selecting a language to study in depth. The foreign language profession must address both these needs if students are to be motivated to stay in foreign language programs long enough to achieve fluency or proficiency.

Today the best curricular vehicle we have for satisfying these needs is the exploratory foreign language offering. And the two people who are best prepared to deal with every facet of exploratory foreign language programs—including administration, organization, content, methodology, teacher training, and evaluation—are Dora Kennedy and William De Lorenzo.

For administrators, curriculum directors, and teachers, this book can serve as a handbook in preparing for and implementing foreign language exploratory experiences. While the prime focus is on the middle or junior high school—because of the unique needs and characteristics of students at this stage in their education—the information in this book applies to all grade levels.

State consultants and the personnel in service offices like that of the Coordinator for School Foreign Languages should welcome this addition to the professional literature, for this book brings us up to date; provides us with models; gives us guidelines, processes, and resources; and points us in positive directions for the future.

There is a great emphasis today on excellence in education. To achieve excellence in foreign language education, we must address the needs of learners first as they approach new disciplines and later at various stages of their development. This book will prove to be invaluable for foreign language educators in meeting the needs of all students studying or preparing to study a foreign language. The road to fluency or proficiency, as this book will convince you, begins with exploration.

Lorraine A. Strasheim
Coordinator for School Foreign Languages
Office of School Programs
Indiana University

Complete Guide to

EXPLORATORY FOREIGN
LANGUAGE PROGRAMS

Chapter 1

Exploratory Courses: What and Why

Although the idea of exploratory foreign language courses emerged in American education several decades ago, their "rebirth" offers a challenge for curriculum planning since there have been few guidelines for establishing such programs. The exploratory course represents a different dimension for the foreign language offering; hence there is a need for development of a cohesive curriculum.

This book defines the exploratory foreign language concept, both historically and as it currently applies to middle/junior high schools, and as an aid to teachers and administrators, outlines the goals, objectives, content, and organization of exploratory programs. The book's major components are based on a national survey, the body of considerable literature of the past on the subject, investigation of several program models, and personal experience in implementing an exploratory course in a large school system.

What Is an Exploratory Course?

In order to establish a common perspective, let us explain in detail the three terms most germane to the exploratory concept: exploratory, general language, and language potpourri or trial language study course.

Exploratory: Within the context of the foreign language field, this word is used as a generic term for courses designed to carry out one or more language-and-culture functions in the cognitive, affective, and psychomotor domains, such as:

1. Introducing pupils to the phenomenon of language, its sounds, signs, structure; its development; language families, differences and similarities among specific languages

2. Helping pupils improve their understanding of English vocabulary and structure, through the study of roots, affixes, and through linguistic comparisons

1

3. Having pupils learn about a variety of cultures as related to the languages explored; their historical as well as current role in helping to build this country

4. Providing experiences in learning to understand and say in varying degrees actual samples of different foreign languages, i.e., "trying-out" experiences

5. Teaching specific techniques associated with foreign language study

6. Leading pupils to explore the role of foreign languages in careers and in their own career development

7. Fostering appreciation of other tongues, peoples, and cultures, with pride in one's own heritage

8. Creating a positive attitude toward foreign language study, building a readiness for it, and helping pupils make an informed choice in electing a sequential language program.

[Bourque, 1976, p. 11; Brannon and Cox, 1976, p. 166; Enwall et al., 1975, p. 203; Fearing and Grittner, 1974, pp. 1-2; Prince George's County, 1975, pp. 1; 96-102]

Although the exploratory course can be implemented at any educational level, nearly all courses of this nature, designated as exploratory, appear prior to senior high school, usually in middle or junior high school (Fryer, 1975, p. 29).

Under the broad classification of *exploratory*, courses are designated by various titles, depending on the emphases or main thrust of the content.

General Language: This term refers to exploratory courses that stress functions *1, 2, 3, 7,* and *8,* above, with the possible inclusion of functions *4* and *5* as part of a component on learning a foreign language (Bourque, 1976, p. 11; Brannon and Cox, 1976, p. 167); or as a series of skill development activities involving one or more specific languages (Fearing and Grittner, 1974, p. 3). The National Council of State Supervisors of Foreign Languages uses the term "Language Overview" (Enwall et al., 1975, p. 2).

Language Potpourri or *Trial Language Study Course:* (Enwall et al., 1975, p. 3). Exploratory courses characterized by this term emphasize functions *4* and *5* above; some, however, have also designed into their program functions *1-3* and *6-8,* to be infused as the course proceeds (Love and Honig, 1973, pp. 49-55; Prince George's County, 1975, pp. 1, 5, 8, 9).

Responses to a *Survey for Curriculum Development* (see Appendix A), distributed throughout various parts of the country, show that clear distinctions between general language and language potpourri courses are actually theoretical. Most respondents stated that they had combined aspects of both ideas. The conclusion was made that emphases are determined by the proclivities and insights of those designing and implementing these courses, as illustrated below. The following titles are currently, or have been, used to designate exploratory courses:

> General Language and Culture (Stratford, Connecticut)
> Language and Man (Monroe County, Indiana)
> Foreign Language Survey (Omaha, Nebraska)
> Foreign Language Exploratory (Prince George's County, Maryland)
> Foreign Language Appreciation (Baltimore County, Maryland)
> Junior Jet Set (Lilburn, Georgia)
> Foreign Languages Exploratory—FLEX (Topeka, Kansas)
> The Phenomenon of Language (North Hollywood, California)

Most exploratory courses currently being implemented are indeed concerned with acquainting pupils with the nature of language and samples of one or more languages and with raising the level of awareness of world languages and cultures. In the parlance of the language teaching profession, exploratory courses are self-contained or nonsequential, that is, they are not part of a conventional sequence in which a pupil moves from one predefined instructional level to the next. Experiences of an exploratory course can precede formal, sequential language study, or they may stand alone as educationally worthy (Fearing and Grittner, 1974, p. 1; Sims and Hammond, 1981, pp. 28-30).

A Rationale for Exploratory

Increasingly diverse groups of students have become involved in foreign language study (Tursi, 1970, pp. 106-133). This development has resulted primarily from the gradual relaxation of restrictive criteria which had limited enrollment to the linguistically highly able, particularly during the 1960s. The foreign language teaching profession has acknowledged the diversity of needs, aptitudes, and goals of students with interests in languages and cultures, and it has attempted a variety of curricular adaptations and additions to conventional programs.

Foreign language methodologist Wilga Rivers (1975), writing in the March 1975 issue of *Foreign Language Annals*, captured the essence of these trends:

> Foreign language teaching is moving from an elitist to a comprehensive view of its task. As a profession we must consider much more seriously what the study of a foreign language can contribute to the education of all students with their widely diverse abilities, interests and modes of learning. [P. 23]

Exploratory foreign language courses are considered worthy options by both administrators and teachers in helping to provide for necessarily varied programming (Fearing and Grittner, 1974, p. 1). Such courses are particularly compatible with the exploratory goals of the middle school and early junior high school, and it is at these levels that most of the attempts at exploratory programs are taking place (Fearing and Grittner, 1974, pp. 1-3).

Since most American children do not have contact with a foreign language during their elementary school years, an exploratory experience in middle school may provide them with an orientation and readiness for formal language study.

There is also an increasingly broad base of community and parental support for the principle of exploratory programs in foreign languages (Love, 1973, pp. 53, 54; Morrow, 1974, p. 143; Omaggio, 1983, pp. 38, 39).

Nationwide surveys continue to reflect the existence of such programs (Eddy, 1980, p. 45); the American Council on the Teaching of Foreign Languages (ACTFL) and the Northeast Conference have in recent years regularly included sessions on exploratory programs in their annual meetings. The 1983 *Northeast Conference Reports* (pp. 38, 39; 51, 52) include exploratory course descriptions, summarizing the main goals found in most courses and elaborating upon several programs reported in recent literature (Sims and Hammond, 1981, pp. 28-30).

The need for diversification of what Ziegler calls "the monolithic foreign language curriculum" (1974, p. 118) had been recognized by the profession before World War II, and such a movement was indeed under way (Kaulfers, 1942a, p. 6). However, postwar America demanded lengthy foreign language sequences beginning in elementary school. This demand was subsequently reinforced by the advent of the *Sputnik* era, with its concerns for academic rigor. Most school systems strengthened their foreign language offerings by adding upper levels to the sequence and by focusing on listening and speaking as well as reading and writing. Many also added foreign language programs to their elementary schools, usually referred to as FLES (Foreign Language in Elementary School) programs. It was believed that participation in a FLES program would serve as an exploratory experience; however, most FLES programs featured tightly controlled skill-building content, so there was little opportunity to learn concepts *about* language. Furthermore, FLES programs of the 1960s tended to assume that all children involved were ready for intensive, formal instruction in a foreign language.

The revival of the exploratory concept in the 1970s was due in part to the demise of most public school FLES programs and the recognition of the increasingly pluralistic student body (Fearing and Grittner, 1974, p. 1).

At the 1975 session of the annual Northeast Conference on Teaching Foreign Languages, Nelson Brooks proposed that the profession turn its attention to the development of exploratory programs during the 1970s. Brooks's exhortations may have strongly influenced an already flourishing movement. The challenge vis-à-vis such programs lies in curricular development and administrative organization. From the curricular point of view, these programs need a unifying conceptual framework. Since curriculum development in the exploratory context did not continue during the decades between World War II and the present, there is actually little which has been formalized as a suggested body of common concepts to guide schools contemplating the establishment of such programs.

Middle Schools

The development of exploratory foreign language curricula for the middle school must take into account the goals of the institution. Middle schools address the educational needs of older children and early adolescents, ages 10-14, sometimes referred to as "transescents" (Morgan and Williams, 1970, p. 1).

An exploratory foreign language curriculum for the middle school can partially address several needs concurrently:

1. **The Learner:** The need to respond to the intellectual requirements of the transescent learner, "characterized by a desire to investigate, discover, expand and explore a wide range of topics and areas of interest, including the exploration and awareness of the world of work" (Prince George's Task Force, 1973, p. 24).

2. **The Foreign Language Field:** The need to define more precisely the "underdeveloped" exploratory phase of the foreign language curricular spectrum.

3. **The Institution:** The need to provide the middle school with well-organized curricula of an interdisciplinary nature, thus helping to eliminate the "patchwork and add-ons" to the degree that these exist.

Given the exploratory thrust advocated as a significant component of the middle school curriculum, a program of foreign language exploration can not only help to meet the transescent learner's increasing need to investigate new areas of interest, but it can also be a "hands-on" experience in the *career development* process. Thus an exploratory foreign language course would be a part of the career exploration program of a middle school. In addition, however, specific concepts must be infused or "blended into the course fabric," since elementary school programs rarely include foreign languages in their career awareness activities. Therefore, career education will be an important component of the curricular model of an exploratory course presented in subsequent chapters of this text.

Exploratory Courses vis-à-vis Curriculum Development

Examination of a number of curriculum documents, correspondence with several school systems, and discussions at leading conferences warrant the conclusion that although curricular planning for exploratory courses appears adequate with regard to specific skills and processes, it appears weak in philosophical orientation and in structure, that is, in the development of unifying principles or basic ideas which transcend the subject matter. Further, the infusion of career education concepts is rare. It has become evident that curriculum development in this field requires a clearer formulation of some basic unifying concepts in language, culture, and career education. The authors believe that such a formulation can be useful as a frame of reference for those creating new courses of this type or revising existing courses.

Taba (1962, p. 178) reminds developers of curriculum that major concepts should constitute the "recurrent themes" which run through the curriculum in a cumulative and overarching fashion.

This book has involved an investigation to identify overarching concepts for a suggested exploratory foreign language curriculum. As part of this investigation the following questions were posed:

1. What are the most frequently stated goals and objectives of current exploratory foreign language courses?
2. What are the major components of such courses?
   a. What are their common elements?
   b. Which basic linguistic and cultural concepts are either addressed in the content outlines or can be deduced from the material?
   c. What career education concepts, e.g., career awareness, are relatable to the content presented?
3. What are the chief characteristics of past exploratory courses in foreign languages, and which of these characteristics are relevant today?

In seeking answers to these questions, several program models frequently mentioned in the literature were examined, together with their curriculum documents. A national survey on concepts, goals, and objectives was conducted, and the historical development of exploratory programs was traced through the literature.

The information gained in these endeavors has been utilized in the development of a suggested exploratory course model and procedures for teachers and administrators.

The subsequent chapters of this book present the results of the above investigations in detail, including the complete course model. In addition, suggestions are given for teacher training, and lists and samples of materials and resources for the exploratory classroom are provided.

Chapter 2

Exploratory Foreign Language in Retrospect

The exploratory course in foreign languages is an idea enthusiastically conceived in the early decades of this century near the end of World War I, and closely tied at the time to the emerging junior high school.

This chapter documents the beginnings, rise, decline, and eventual rebirth of this type of course in the foreign language curriculum.

Historical Perspective

The earlier literature on the exploratory course spans approximately the years between 1920 and the mid-1950s. Most of the course titles in use today resemble those of that era (Cole, 1937, pp. 361-65; Taylor and Tharp, 1937, p. 89). Although contemporary exploratory courses are often viewed as unique by their designers, detailed descriptions of earlier courses show almost the same components as those of today except that a career development component was lacking. Vocational aspects of foreign language study were frequently highlighted in the professional literature; nevertheless, the inclusion of a vocational dimension was not a goal of most of the exploratory courses. Kaulfers (1942b, pp. 125, 126) described as unusual "an orientation program in language arts" in a California junior high school, in which a general language course included a unit entitled "Language as a Field for Vocational Specialization." From the trends reflected in numerous articles of the times, it is reasonable to conclude that a developmental approach to a prevocational classroom experience is new among the possible functions of the foreign language exploratory course.

Upon examining from a historical perspective the application of the exploratory concept, one is confronted with a basic controversy. This controversy exists between those who advocate early beginning of formal language instruction with lengthy sequence, and those who would first strengthen the general education of the child by broadening experiences through exploration, before "specialization." Brannon and Cox (1976, p.

164) remind their readers that exploratory foreign language courses have been cyclic. The interest in them has risen and fallen in an inverse relationship to the fluctuations in sequential course enrollments, particularly below the senior high school.

Among various publications of the period between World War I and the present examined during this review is *The Modern Language Journal* (1916, et seq.). This journal is the oldest publication in the United States devoted to foreign language pedagogy. Over the decades it has best chronicled the vicissitudes of language programs in American schools. Its pages reflect an abundance of activity in the exploratory field between 1921 and 1956, the year in which it featured its last article on the subject (Levy, 1956, pp. 182-85). It has not documented the reemergence of the exploratory course, though other publications have done so (Born, 1975, p. 94; Bourque, 1976, pp. 10-16; Eddy, 1980, p. 45; Sims and Hammond, 1981, pp. 28-30; Omaggio, 1983, pp. 38, 39, 51, 52; Stern, 1983, pp. 132, 133).

Development of Exploratory Courses

Existing literature indicates that the rise of the exploratory course was closely associated with the rise of the junior high school between 1910 and 1925.

From the time of its establishment, the junior high school was viewed as having an identity problem. What was it to be? An extension of the elementary school upward or of the secondary school downward? The early writings on the junior high school indicated that it was to be neither of these, yet both. The core or unified studies curriculum was inherited from the elementary school; the program of electives was borrowed from the senior high school (Cole, 1937, p. 357). As Cole stated, "It is a distinct educational unit of a transitional nature, guided by what has preceded and by what is to follow, yet independent of both" (1937, p. 351). Nevertheless it was difficult from the beginning for teachers in the academic disciplines to view the institution as anything but preparatory for senior high school courses. The *Eighth Yearbook* of the National Association of Secondary School Principals (1924) addressed the problem thus:

> The first great task was to convince both junior and senior high school faculties that the function of the junior high school was not on the one hand to accelerate pupils, nor on the other to prepare them for senior high school, but to organize and conduct a school which should meet the needs of 7th, 8th, and 9th year age, which should develop those abilities, attitudes, and habits that would find these children at the end of the junior high school years at that point in their general development where children of that age should be. [P. 32]

The document further stated (p. 45) that the seventh and eighth grades should be organized to give pupils a "try-out" in English, mathematics, social sciences, health, shop work, fine arts, general science, commerce, home economics, and *languages.* Such courses were referred to as "broadening and finding" courses (Kaulfers, 1942a, p. 298).

Although the rise of exploratory courses was closely associated with the establishment of the junior high school, a confluence of forces affected the curricula of both junior and senior high schools. A brief analysis of these forces follows.

Dramatic changes in the senior high school

In *The Teaching of Modern Foreign Languages in the United States,* Coleman (1929, p. 2 et seq.) documents the various studies and surveys commissioned up to that time to help determine the place of foreign languages in American education: goals, methods of teaching, and content. From the 1898 report of the *Committee of Twelve,* appointed by the Modern Language Association, to the 17 volumes produced by the *Modern Foreign Language Study,* which was sponsored by the American Council on Education (1924-1928), conclusions and recommendations remained consistently oriented toward reading as the main objective in teaching modern foreign languages. The two-year course became established by school administrators as the norm throughout the country.

Examination of all the issues of the *Modern Language Journal* during its first two decades of existence reveals mounting preoccupation with the value of the foreign language course for the academically less able. An increasingly broader segment of youth was entering both the junior and senior high schools and in ever expanding numbers. Coleman (1929) described the situation vis-à-vis the senior high school, which prior to the early 1900s served mainly as an academy for the preparation of college-bound students:

> After the Spanish War and the great thrust of industrial expansion which followed it, the cry that the high school was the "People's University" swept from the Central West eastward, and ambitious school administrators began to demand that colleges cease to dictate the program of the secondary school.

The sheer weight of the growing masses forced open the doors of secondary education. [P. 2]

A second great thrust occurred after World War I when large numbers of young men, including veterans, entered the high school.

During the following several decades foreign language teachers, who had been accustomed to academically strong students, continued to express concern that so many might experience failure in their classes. The fact that students were expected to achieve proficiency in reading a foreign language, know its grammar, and be able to render acceptable English translations—all within a two-year training period—led to the advocacy of "preliminary" or exploratory courses for the lower level of the high school (including ninth grade), with the sequential foreign language course reserved for the last two years (Kaulfers, 1936, p. 750; Lindquist, 1930, p. 285).

The following passages from the *Modern Language Journal* bring into focus both the frustrations of the foreign language teachers of the time and their discomfort at having to cope with "a new day."

If we eliminate through prognosis tests or otherwise (exploratory courses) a small part, usually less than 10%, of the students who present themselves for a modern language, two years will yield a practical reading speed. [Roehm, 1931, p. 228.]

It is the *hoi polloi* that we must be concerned with. The boy and girl of the laboring class are on the whole too exhausted physically and mentally to harbor any craving for reading which would entail any mental exertion. . . . It is out of the question to expect them to read in a foreign tongue, even if they were able to. [Waldman, 1931, p. 233.]

Beginning in the 1920s there was a movement in senior high school toward the creation of self-contained, or terminal, courses in "national cultures," with the technicalities of the foreign language forming only a small part of the content (Kaulfers, 1938, p. 337, and 1942b, pp. 135-236). These courses were sometimes called "Orientation Courses in Language Arts"; "Preliminary Foreign Language Courses"; and "Introduction to Languages and Cultures" (Kaulfers, 1928, pp. 281-83 and 1938, p. 737). The leadership of this movement was based in California. In the Midwest, Lindquist of the Detroit Public Schools was the leading advocate of the General Language "laboratory" course (1930, pp. 285-89), meeting similar needs.

In summary, exploratory foreign language courses emerged not only as part of the curriculum for the new junior high school but also as senior high school courses (including ninth grade) to fulfill two purposes from the point of view of their organizers:

1. To provide a positive foreign language experience for students who were expected to fail the conventional course

2. To eliminate these students from the conventional course by providing the exploratory alternative.

Lindquist stated that the "General Language course serves to eliminate the linguistically unfit, thus diminishing failures" (1930, p. 289).

The building of readiness to study a foreign language, a strong component of current exploratory courses, was not emphasized in the early literature, although it was not overlooked completely. Its consideration was overridden by the concern for helping students avoid failure by eliminating them from the sequential foreign language course.

Emergence of the junior high school exploratory course

The junior high school curriculum was developed during those years of drastic change in the senior high school. The gradual phasing out of elementary school foreign language programs, which had flourished in the 1920s and earlier, provided impetus for the establishment of elective foreign language courses in grades seven and eight (Bagster-Collins et al., 1930, p. 46).

The inclusion of foreign languages in the early junior high school years spurred a heated controversy between administrators and some foreign language teachers, and among the teachers themselves. These differences were part of the larger controversy over the exploratory and preparatory functions of the junior high school (Cole, 1937, pp. 356-57). Those teachers who agreed with the pedagogical theory that young students did not need and were not interested in specialized subject matter worked toward the development of orientation or exploratory courses (Cole, 1937, p. 358). Administrators were, in general, supportive of this movement because it was more compatible with their philosophy of the junior high school, and because they were concerned about the high level of attrition in the foreign language classes.

In the final report of the *Modern Foreign Language Study*, Coleman (1929) made the following observations in the section dealing with the junior high school:

Children at this age will profit little by formal grammar instruction. . .work would be more profitable in "general language," and introduction through reading and realia to the life and civilization of the countries. [P. 35]

In this document, known in the field as the "Coleman Report," Coleman admitted that the junior high school curriculum was in a state of flux. He referred to reports from administrators citing such small classes in third year (grade 9) that they questioned the advisability of continuing the offering. A director of foreign languages in a midwestern city was quoted by Coleman as follows:

> We do not find that pupils take more French because they begin it earlier. We are now contemplating dropping all foreign languages from eighth grade and substituting a year of general language which will lead to any foreign language in grade nine. [P. 41]

On the other hand, dissenting voices were heard in an editorial comment in the May 1928 issue of the *Modern Language Journal:*

> Language study in junior high school should be a definite object of study and research on the part of our profession. The subject is much disputed and objective facts are rare and inconclusive. One difficulty results from the fact that junior high school work has in many cases not been correlated with language study in the senior high school. . . .
>
> Considering the ease with which young children learn to speak a foreign idiom, and the genuine pleasure which it nearly always affords them, do we do well to postpone foreign language study? [Morgan, pp. 658-59]

The effect of this tug-of-war between exploratory and preparatory functions was also being felt as of this writing among organizers of middle schools. In 1975 the National Council of State Supervisors of Foreign Languages stated in a position paper on exploratory courses:

> Some foreign language educators favor the Level I course over the exploratory course in the middle grades; they point out however, that the implementation of Level I in the middle school creates certain problems. . .articulation with the senior high school can be critical. [Enwall, p. 6]

Despite the controversy over exploratory and preparatory functions of grades seven and eight, thrust toward exploratory courses in foreign language grew through the 1920s and 1930s.

Content and purposes of course identified

From the earliest article encountered (Cline, 1921, pp. 435-43), through numerous references in subsequent decades prior to the late fifties, descriptions of content and purpose were surprisingly consistent, regardless of geographic location of the program. The methodology advocated appeared to have been influenced by the language arts component of the elementary school curriculum (that is, child centered and activity oriented); the content was usually modeled after the previously mentioned orientation courses advocated for the lower levels of senior high school. Highly respected educators in the foreign language field were among its organizers and advocates, for example, Blancké, Cole, Kaulfers, Lindquist, and Tharp, among others.

Because these courses were new to most teachers and since they did not fit the mold of conventional foreign language courses, the literature of the time reflected the need to describe them in detail.

Figure 2-1 incorporates some of the most significant of the numerous descriptions appearing between 1921 and 1956. It was not intended to be exhaustive; rather the intent was to reflect the chronology of the exploratory course as a curricular phenomenon.

Author	Date	Pertinent Data
Cline	1921	"A general language laboratory* course"— schools of Richmond, Indiana—organized 1918.
Snedaker	1928	"Pre-language" or "finding and broadening courses"—Oklahoma City—organized 1926.
Wehr	1930	"General language." Among most detailed. Features program—West Hartford, Connecticut—organized 1915. Claimed to be the first exploratory program in the country.
Kaulfers	1928 1936 1936 1937 1938 1942	"Orientation courses in national cultures"— heavier cultural emphasis than most "general language" programs. Various schools in California—organized in 1925.
Lindquist	1930 1937 1938 1940 1945	"General language"—Detroit Public Schools— organized C. 1920. Most enduring and most frequently described exploratory program.
Michie	1938	"General language curriculum"—several Wyoming schools—date of first implementation not specified.

*The term "laboratory" in the context of exploratory courses meant that instructional materials were created by teacher and pupils. (Cline, 1921, p. 435).

Voze	1939	"Foreign language exploration"—Champaign, Illinois—organized 1923.
Blancké	1939	"General language"—Philadelphia—date of first implementation not specified.
Tharp	1939 1940 1943	"General language—appreciation courses in study of foreign languages."
Brenman	1942	"Civilization courses"—Newark, New Jersey—date of first implementation not specified.
Hutchinson	1946	"General language—elementary linguistics"—advocated for postwar language programs.
Finocchiaro	1952	"General language"—Brooklyn—organized 1945.
Daley	1953	"Language 8"—Syracuse, New York—organized 1952.
Gordon	1953	"General language"—Ohio schools—date not specified.
Forsheit	1954	"Consumer education in language"—advocacy of foreign language in the core curriculum.
Wasley	1955	"Exploratory course in modern languages"—campus school—New York State College for Teachers—organized 1953.
Levy	1956	"General language"—New York City—organized 1945 (by 1955, only two schools were implementing course).

Figure 2-1. Chronology of representative descriptive articles on exploratory foreign language, 1921-1956.

Although Kaulfers and Lindquist were the most prolific of the writers on exploratory between 1921 and 1945, Wehr's description (1930, pp. 194-206) appeared to be the most concise yet thorough of all those encountered.

Wehr undertook a nationwide study of the general language course for the Classical Association of the Middle West and South. A schema summarizing her report to the Association's Committee on Junior High School Latin is presented in Figure 2-2. (Teachers of the classics have generally been supportive of exploratory courses since Latin/Greek elements are usually a significant component of them.)

Exploratory   GENERAL LANGUAGE   Introductory

Evolution of language and orientation to foreign language
DEFINITION   • Course placed in junior high school
             • Semester or year's duration
             • Development and evolution of language

> English-history/elements
> comparative philology (linguistics, etymology)

             • Exploratory lessons/foreign languages
             • Foreign peoples—civilization, manners, customs

OBJECTIVES   • *Orientation—guidance*
             foreign language lessons
             pupil discovery: aptitudes, interests, preferences; for informed decisions

             • *Academic learnings*
             Imparting knowledge: about English, about language, about languages, about cultures

             • *Appreciation*
             other people and languages

CONTENT   • *Integrating material*
             language/social studies/music/art

Figure 2-2. Schema of prevailing general language/exploratory course.*

In the same document, Wehr (pp. 199-200) reported that 24 states had exploratory programs as of 1930. Analogies between other "general" subjects of the developing junior high school and general language continued to be drawn (p. 195).

---

*As described by Wehr (1930, pp. 194-206).

Wehr also found (pp. 200-01) that there was greater use of teacher-made and pupil-made materials than was the practice in conventional language classes. However, Wehr and other writers pointed out that most programs relied on one of the six available textbooks in the field for their basic structure (Cole, 1937, pp. 620-21). The first of these texts, *General Language*, by Leonard and Cox, appeared in 1925. By the early 1940s, 11 texts on general language had been published. (See annotated list in Appendix B.) Only Lindquist's text, *General Language—English and Its Foreign Relations*, prevailed until the late 1960s. As of 1980 it was out of print; however, most existing exploratory programs have gleaned ideas and information from it since no contemporary text has been available.

In addition to Lindquist's, the following early junior high school exploratory texts were examined:

General Language (Bugbee et al., 1926)
Your Language (Cline, 1930)
Principles of Language (Blancké, 1935; revised 1953)

Textbooks that aimed at exploratory programs, as well as works on methodology, generally concurred with the content advocated (Cole, 1937, pp. 620-21). Wehr's description is reflective of the content commonly espoused (see Figure 2-2).

Evaluation

There was continuing concern over the future of the exploratory course, the extent of its implementation, and whether it really helped students. Its expansion continued until the late 1930s when it probably reached its zenith.

Blancké (1939, p. 73) was critical of the sampling type of course but favored the general language approach. He feared that the sampling experience might be deceptive in perhaps misrepresenting the nature of foreign language study.

In 1937 Taylor and Tharp presented an elaborate evaluative report on the topic (pp. 83-91). It drew heavily from a monograph by Eddy (1932), commissioned by the Department of Interior for the National Survey of Secondary Education. In this monograph Eddy had summarized the status of exploratory courses as part of the junior high school section of the report.

In addition, however, Taylor and Tharp (pp. 84-88) had submitted a lengthy questionnaire to all schools known to be using the general language texts then available and to other schools reporting exploratory programs. They found an overwhelmingly positive attitude toward such programs; the controversy over the prognosis value of the course had lessened in favor of orientation and terminal purposes, enriching the curriculum both for students who planned to enroll in a foreign language and for those who did not.

The responses also showed that success or failure of the course depended on its purposes, the point of view, and the attitude of those who taught and administered it (p. 88). In spite of the various texts that attempted to pinpoint content, Taylor and Tharp concluded that objectives, techniques, and content for such a course had not yet been established and that the term "general" should be changed since it could connote "something of little value."

It is noteworthy that more than four decades later content still varied somewhat from one program to another, and the term "general language" persists. However, the preoccupation with the minutiae of content may have been unwarranted. That a national consensus was emerging with regard to the nature of the course becomes obvious with the advantage of hindsight. In Wehr's terms (1930, p. 196), there was a coalescing of objectives around orientation—guidance, academic learnings, and appreciation of cultures—an emergence of overriding concepts which all appeared to endorse.

Literature on the topic revealed that evaluative studies have not been a forte of exploratory programs. With the exception of Love and Honig (1973, pp. 49-55), the main body of the literature is characterized by surveys, program descriptions, anecdotal passages, including empirical data revealing how students were aided by this course.

Voze (1938) prefaced a detailed account of the program in a junior high school in Champaign, Illinois, with the following statement:

> Exploratory courses have been introduced to help guide students intelligently into subject fields which are within their capacities and interests. . . .Exploratory language work belongs in the junior high school.[P. 22]

Although a number of articles on the subject appeared in the 1940s, Voze (1939, pp. 22-27) captured the essence of most of the exploratory programs being implemented on the eve of World War II.

The salient features of her description are summarized below. The course was called *Introductory Foreign Language.*

Aims

According to Voze, the aims of the course coincided with the global aims of the junior high school, which were:

- To help individuals discover themselves
- To guide and direct pupils in choices which might develop their maximum potential.

Thus, the course aimed to:

- Assist students in wise selection of a language for study
- Benefit students who "could not pass a conventional foreign language course."

Content

- Survey of language and development of English
- Material in English about various cultures
- Actual lessons in each language which might be elected later.

Organization

- Elective in grade 8
- Three times weekly for two semesters
- Three teachers presented the work of six units
- Students were given credit for the course
- All students passed the course, even though some did poorly in the foreign language component.

Evaluation—outcomes

- Development of language sense
- Ability to recognize and distinguish among some foreign languages through comparison of forms and sounds
- Acquisition of background material, with subsequent interest in foreign peoples and lands
- Ability to choose a language wisely.

At the end of the first year of implementation, *20* out of *30* students enrolled in a foreign language course. Twelve out of these 20 received the same letter grade as they had received in the exploratory course (p. 26).

Voze pointed out that there were no tests for validity for such a course. She attested to the enthusiasm of the community and school (p. 26).

The preceding description typified both the exploratory course as it had evolved up to 1939 and those courses which endured into the postwar era.

The eventual decline of the early exploratory course

In retrospect it becomes clear that the war marked the beginning of the slow decline of the early exploratory course. Almost abruptly the language journals reflected the national shortage of linguistic resources and the consequent thrust toward military language training programs at the college level.

The lack of vigorous support in teacher training institutions may have also contributed to the eclipse of the exploratory approach. In 1930, Wehr had called for "provision on the part of the schools of higher learning for preparing teachers to teach general language" (p. 206). Cole (1937, pp. 368-69) had also expressed concern over the breadth of knowledge and preparation required for teaching such a course.

However, since the exploratory concept did not originate at the college or university level but rather had been a "grass roots" movement, there was apprehension in some college level language departments that it might displace conventional courses in the secondary school (McGalliard et al., 1941, pp. 892-93). Therefore, with a few exceptions—e.g., the course instituted by Muller (1944, pp. 425-28) at Adelphi College in Garden City, New York—little effort appeared to be expended in the establishment of preservice courses of this nature. Furthermore, the contribution of the colleges to the in-service education of exploratory teachers in the field was minimal.

In the early 1950s, there was a brief flurry of activity representing the culmination of a long-range attempt on the part of some teachers to incorporate foreign languages into the mainstream of the junior high school. The thrust had been to establish a link, through the exploratory course, with the strong trend toward "integrated programs," e.g., the core curriculum (Fouts, 1954, pp. 9-21). Advocates of this approach had enthusiastically embraced the idea of integrating foreign languages with social studies, English, music, and art (Finocchiaro, 1952, p. 20; Forsheit, 1954, p. 356; Gordon, 1953, p. 160; Sandow, 1952, p. 20). This trend too was engulfed in the ensuing audiolingual movement, which was itself reinforced toward the end of the decade by a renewed stress on more structured curricula in the wake of *Sputnik*.

In summary, the following factors were considered as contributing to the gradual eclipse of the exploratory course in the late 1940s and early 1950s:

1. The trend toward the strengthening of sequential programs as a reaction to the World War II experience, which had revealed a less than adequate provision for foreign language education in the nation's schools

2. The returning veterans who demanded an expansion of foreign language programs in their communities

3. The general lack of support in college language departments

4. The lack of consensus in the language teaching profession vis-à-vis the exploratory approach

5. The emphasis on depth in the academic disciplines at all school levels, as a nation reacted to *Sputnik* with the feeling that its schools were not doing an adequate job.

In anticipation of an "approaching foreign language boom," as had been predicted by Tharp (1943, p. 460) and others, efforts to document the exploratory movement diminished, with the result that during the 1960s references to these programs were rare.

The Exploratory Cycle

The exploratory course did not disappear completely from the secondary school scene. Once the idea had been conceived, the profession was reluctant to abandon it totally. Even as some school systems were phasing it out, others, though fewer in number, were phasing it in (Daley, 1953, p. 38; Levy, 1956, p. 182; Wasley, 1955, p. 187). Thus, during the 1950s and 1960s there were a few schools throughout the country that attempted to preserve it. There were some teachers who were just discovering its value (Bigelow, 1963). Insofar as could be determined, Detroit was the only public school system in which the exploratory course had endured from its inception around 1920, albeit with slowly declining enrollments.[1]

Harbingers of Approaching Revival

In conferences on the future of foreign language education held during World War II and during the decade immediately following, the exploratory course was usually paid lip service, if not embraced so enthusiastically as in previous times (Hutchinson, 1946, p. 261; Olinger, 1946, p. 3; Tharp, 1943c, p. 326).

The Modern Language Association, without advocating the establishment of a general language course, did endorse several of its objectives in its Policy Statement, in the *Modern Langugage Journal*, November 1956:

. . .a new understanding of language progressively revealing to the pupil the structure of language and giving him a perspective on

---

[1]Response from Detroit Public Schools to *Survey for Curriculum Development.*

English as well as an increased vocabulary and greater effectiveness in expression. [P. 409]

During the 1960s the profession was steeped in the audiolingual movement, a fact well documented in the annual *Northeast Conference Reports* of 1959-1964. Even though many had apparently rejected the idea of exploratory courses, a few continued to recognize the need for breadth as well as depth. In 1966 Pei expressed a view which was held by an extremely small segment of the profession:

> . . .one feature I would strongly urge for all, without exception—a general language survey course of one semester or one year, prior to the actual selection of a specific language, to familiarize the students with the language situation throughout the world, the chief languages spoken, their location, the extent of their speaking populations. . .along with a sampling of those which the school offers. [P. 74]

Thus, Pei reverted to his strong earlier advocacy of the exploratory course (1936, p. 376). Rivers (1968, p. 8) also included among her objectives for foreign language programs the need to increase the student's understanding of language in general.

Trends reflected in evaluative instruments

An instrument which should mirror the state of the art in the disciplines of the secondary school is the *Evaluative Criteria*, published since 1940, by the National Study of Secondary School Evaluation,[2] and utilized by most secondary schools for their decennial evaluation and accreditation. Even though it is considered a senior high school instrument, it is significant that both the 1940 and 1960 editions of the foreign language section under *Nature of Offerings* listed "introductory courses which provide opportunity to compare modes of expression in other languages with those in English" (*Evaluative Criteria*, 1960, p. 124). There was also a reference to the provision of "orientation" in the beginning level courses (p. 124).

Paradoxically, the 1964 revision of the *Evaluative Criteria*, intended for use in the 1970s, eliminated the above references in favor of exclusive emphasis on the fundamental skills in sequential courses. No concessions were made to the emerging movement toward greater curricular flexibility.

---

[2]In 1970, the name changed to National Study of School Evaluation.

On the other hand, the *Evaluative Criteria* for *Junior High School/Middle School,* under its category for all disciplines entitled *Nature of the Program,* posed this question: "In what ways is exploration provided for each student enrolled in this subject?" (1970, p. 64).

Factors contributing to a new ascendancy

During the late 1960s many factors which had been deemphasized during the rise of the audiolingual movement surfaced into the mainstream of thought of the foreign language establishment. These developments, whose influence continues today, established a climate conducive to the reestablishment of the idea of breadth, prelanguage experiences, and enlarged cultural content. They are summarized here:

1. The disillusionment of teachers and students with the extreme adherence to the audiolingual philosophy which had focused almost exclusively on the technical aspects of language training at the lower levels, with negligible attention to the richness of other aspects of the target culture. This disillusionment was buttressed by learning theorists who had criticized the Skinnerian (Stimulus-Response) approach to foreign language learning on which many audiolingual procedures had been based (Carroll, 1966, pp. 36-37; Chomsky, 1966, p. 43; Rivers, 1964, pp. 24-25, 117).

2. The high attrition rates of students enrolled in programs which had been designed to provide long sequences (Tursi, 1970, p. 115).

3. A return to an integrative approach to education, spawning an increase in interdisciplinary programs and activities (Jensen, 1974, pp. 63-64; Warriner, 1971, pp. 128-29).

4. A gradual shift to a middle school concept for the preadolescent, with its attendant interdisciplinary curricular philosophy, and its emphasis on exploration (DiVirgilio, 1973, p. 22).

5. A veritable ground swell for the inclusion of way-of-life culture in all phases of foreign language teaching (Brooks, 1964, pp. 82-96; 1966, pp. 1-4; 1968, pp. 204-17; Nostrand, 1974, pp. 263-327).

6. The shedding of the elitist stance by the foreign language profession at the secondary school level, thus involving wider student participation (Tursi, 1970, pp. 110-11).

7. The career education movement which has fostered the idea of academic as well as vocational exploration (Hoyt, 1975, p. 60).

8. The reassessment of educational practices, motivated in part by the effects of societal upheavals on youth, resulted in more curricular options and flexibility to meet individual needs and interests (Love and Honig, 1973, p. xvi; Tursi, 1970, pp. 9, 99; Warriner, 1971, p. 129).

9. The erosion of college foreign language requirements, though having negative effects, also served as a "liberating" force spurring the secondary school to attempt less orthodox arrangements in foreign language program development (Modern Language Association, 1973, p. 5).

10. The "National Foreign Language Program for the 1970's," a position paper by the Modern Language Association again called for the development of courses about human language (1973, p. 12).

11. The general acceptance and application of goals and performance objectives for foreign language students and programs provided a framework for the organization of nonsequential courses. This approach has facilitated the establishment of course boundaries, with a high degree of specificity (Steiner, 1975, pp. 1-13).

Given the foregoing conditions and because foreign languages had become a relatively isolated phenomenon in elementary schools (Fryer, 1975, p. 26), the time seemed ripe for the establishment of an interdisciplinary program that would provide another dimension in the development of language arts and cultural concepts in grades six through eight. A program of this type could also build readiness for formal study of a foreign language.

Whereas the aforementioned trends fostered the creation of minicourses of various types in the senior high school, in the middle/junior high school the profession returned to the exploratory course (Fryer, 1975, p. 28). The cyclic nature of the exploratory offering is shown in Figure 2-3.

Current Status of Exploratory Programs

Recent literature is not lacking in references to exploratory programs and in their advocacy (e.g., Omaggio, 1983, pp. 38, 39; NASSP, 1980). However, old controversies have not entirely disappeared. The basic controversy still centers around how best to introduce children to foreign languages when dealing with a formal classroom setting.

Relative Interest in Exploratory Programs as Revealed by the Literature

Approximate
Time Periods: 1920-1930   1940-1945   1946-1956   1957-1969   1970-1980s

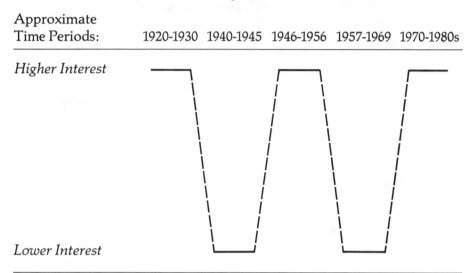

Higher Interest

Lower Interest

Figure 2-3.   The emerging exploratory cycle: 1920-1980s.
                 Pertinent historical factors:
                 1920-1939   - Increase in junior high schools
                 1940-1945   - World War II—emphasis on military
                                    language training
                 1946-1956   - Postwar resurgence of programs
                 1957-1969   - Audiolingual era
                 1970-1980s   - Era of educational diversity

Those who believe that children are enriched and helped by the exploratory experience feel that the following obstacles may still exist:

1. The belief among *some* foreign language professionals, administrators, curriculum planners, and possibly school board members that exploratory language courses are not as viable as the more traditional sequential courses, and that they are not worthy of the same academic status.

2. The conviction that there is no need for alternatives to a sequential foreign language program or for a presequential program in early middle/junior high school.

Despite these real and perceived obstacles, there are clear indications that the current exploratory movement is growing. The authors base this statement on the following evidence:

1. The increasing number of related sessions presented at national and regional pedagogical conferences: the *ACTFL* annual meetings in 1982 and 1983, as well as throughout the 1970s; *Northeast Conference* from 1981 to 1984. The consistent support of the concept by these organizations.

2. The frequent inquiries received from other school systems by established programs for assistance in establishing such classes, e.g., Prince George's County, Maryland, and Fairfax County, Virginia.

3. The inclusion of exploratory foreign language in the project of the National Education Association, *Education in the 80s,* in collaboration with ACTFL. (See *Bibliography* at the back of this text.)

4. Detailed descriptions of exploratory curricula in recent literature (Omaggio, 1983, pp. 38, 39; Stern, 1983, pp. 120-46; Hawkins, 1981, pp. 236-39; 292-306). (See chapter 7 of this text.)

5. Trends as revealed by surveys described on the following pages.

Recent Exploratory Surveys

In the fall of 1979, the Northeast Conference conducted a nationwide survey on the status of foreign language teaching. Of the 732 secondary school foreign language teacher respondents, 23.1 percent indicated that they had some type of exploratory program in the junior high schools of their districts. Of the 335 colleges and universities which responded, 20.3 percent indicated that they offered an "Introduction to Language" college level course (Eddy, 1980, p. 45).

An informal nationwide survey by the authors early in 1984 revealed that the exploratory language movement continues to grow. Inquiries were made by state and an approximate 70 percent return was realized. Out of 36 states responding, only five indicated that they had no exploratory programs.

The authors' informal survey also revealed that hundreds of programs exist throughout the country and that some states have only recently begun to keep statistics on these classes, while others do not keep such figures. Several state consultants, contacted by telephone, indicated that they are including exploratory courses in their new foreign language guidelines.

A Fluid State of the Art

Some may believe that it is once again the eleventh hour in the exploratory cycle. Various studies of secondary education (e.g., "A Nation at Risk," the President's Commission on Excellence in Education, April 1983) have recommended foreign language study with an earlier beginning. The movement to highlight the need for developing and measuring foreign language proficiency has been spearheaded by ACTFL with the publication of the *ACTFL Provisional Proficiency Guidelines* (Higgs, 1984, pp. 219-27). These two developments may signal to some that only sequential programs are viable in the middle or junior high schools. However, the authors' continuing investigations reveal two important developments:

1. The exploratory concept is clearly an enduring "grass roots" movement, based on the perceived needs of children at certain stages of educational development.

2. The exploratory concept appears to be evolving in such a manner as to render academic the question of *either* exploratory *or* sequential. Three examples of this trend are:

    a. Some educators have proposed that exploratory curricula could be incorporated into beginning sequential courses as precourse material or as a course concurrent with the sequential. They consider the content of exploratory curricula too important to ignore (Stern, 1983, p. 132; Hawkins, 1981, pp. 236, 237).

    b. A "bridging" course or experience between the mother tongue and foreign language study helps to address developmental needs of children, whether in elementary or middle/junior high school (Hawkins, 1981, p. 236).

    c. A middle school exploratory course can be organized around languages not offered in the local FLES program—middle school pupils might enroll in such a course while continuing their sequential language study.[3]

Current literature contains descriptions of outstanding programs that are presently being implemented in a variety of schools (Omaggio, 1983, pp. 38, 39). Exploratory courses of this "new" cycle, however, were first implemented in the early 1970s. Several historically representative models are described in the next chapter.

---

[3]See description of Rochester program, in chapter 3. Also, the idea set forth in item *c* above was mentioned to one of the authors by a European visitor while visiting the program in Prince George's County, Maryland.

Chapter 3

Basic Exploratory Program Models

In this chapter we will examine seven program models that originated in the earlier days of the current exploratory renaissance (1970-1976):

- Topeka, Kansas
- Stratford, Connecticut
- Rochester, New York
- Baltimore County, Maryland
- Fairfax County, Virginia
- Monroe County, Indiana
- Prince George's County, Maryland

Although current literature contains examples of exploratory programs throughout the country, these programs were among the original models. They were chosen for detailed study for the following reasons:

- They reflect a variety of basic organizational formats on which subsequent programs were modeled.
- They have been among the most frequently cited in the literature.
- In spite of the vicissitudes of funding and despite philosophical shifts, most of them have endured and are increasing in influence both locally and nationally.

The following aspects of each program will be presented:

Course title	Performance objectives
Year established	Materials used
Grade level	Methodology
Course type and duration	Organization
Main goals	Evaluation

Information about the programs was obtained through school system documents, references in the literature, authors' personal knowledge, and conversations with program coordinators.

These programs may serve as models for those contemplating establishment of exploratory courses.

Although the Stratford program has been modified and the Monroe County course was discontinued because of funding problems, these programs remain worthy models.

Topeka Public Schools

The first of the revived exploratory course models was organized in 1970 by the public schools of Topeka, Kansas. The Topeka foreign language program was highlighted by the National Association of Secondary School Principals in its *Curriculum Report* of May 1980 (pp. 9, 10). The following description is based on Love and Honig (1973, pp. 49-55) and on information provided by the course designer, who was also the foreign language supervisor of the Topeka schools.

Course title: Foreign Languages Exploratory (FLEX)

Year established: 1970-1971

Grade level: Seventh and eighth

Course duration: Varies from six weeks to one year

Course type: Fusion of general language and language potpourri

Languages: French, German, Russian, Spanish, Latin, Chinese, and BASIC computer language

Main goals: As stated in the school system document:

1. To give each student personal experience in a foreign language before decision making

2. To introduce (not master) the field of foreign languages

3. To have each student experience the mental discipline involved in foreign language learning

4. To convey the notion that studying foreign languages involves study of cultures.

Student performance objectives:

Students will:

1. Learn to recognize both aurally and visually each target language (or family of languages explored)

2. Be able to count (under a hundred); use numerals in simple arithmetic problems; tell time, and give the date

3. Learn to use greetings and parting expressions in simple conversation

4. Use the target language to describe simple geographic facts of the countries involved

5. Respond to basic commands given in the target language

6. Learn names of everyday classroom articles in each language explored

7. Become acquainted with various grammatical idiosyncrasies of each language.

Materials used:

1. Text: *General Language,* "English and Its Foreign Relations," Holt, Rinehart and Winston, 1968

2. Locally developed materials for each target language

3. *Why Study Foreign Languages?* (filmstrip/tape) American Council on the Teaching of Foreign Languages

4. Appropriate commercial materials.

Methodology:

1. Mostly teacher directed

2. Discussion and audiolingual strategies

3. Use of visuals.

Implementation: The original basic format of the course was as follows:

General philosophy (introductory phase)—three weeks (nature of language; families of languages, etc.)

Introduction of a different foreign language/culture at six-week intervals—30 weeks

Comparative analysis—Three weeks (summary of learnings; comparisons among languages explored)

Content—See list of student performance objectives. These apply to all languages explored and constitute the main body of content.*

*Some of the above varies at present because of district reorganization.

Organization: FLEX classes in the six junior high schools and six middle schools of Topeka were scheduled to run simultaneously so that teachers could be rotated every six weeks where possible. One exception was the teacher who taught all five languages in one school. Generally each FLEX teacher was responsible for only one language. Some traveling assignments varied.

For each class, the teacher who taught the first foreign language taught the introductory phase of the course. The final session (comparative analysis) was taught by the last language teacher (Love and Honig, 1973, p. 53).

Junior high school principals were responsible for enrolling incoming seventh- and eighth-grade students in the FLEX. In some middle schools, FLEX was required; in others, it was an elective.

Evaluation: Three aspects of evaluation were addressed by the school system: pupil performance, program effectiveness, and pupil opinion. Each is summarized below.

1. **Pupil performance**

   a. A special FLEX report card is distributed at the end of each language phase, listing the following categories: *S* (Satisfactory), *S−* (Satisfactory, with reservations), and *U* (Unsatisfactory).

   b. Evaluation is based on daily work, conversations, and cultural projects.

   c. One middle school credit is granted, provided the pupil completes at least four phases out of six.

2. **Program effectiveness**

   a. Parent and community reactions are continually sought.

   b. *Growth of program*
      1) The program expanded from two pilot schools to all junior high schools, on a voluntary basis.

      2) Principals consider the program worthwhile.

   c. Empiric evidence shows that FLEX "graduates" did better in level I than non-FLEX pupils (observed during the years when not all schools were participating).

   d. Formal evaluative study (see below)

3. Pupil opinion

A questionnaire in which students respond to:
a. which language they liked most and least

b. the difficulty of each language (for them)

c. which language they would like to continue.

Synopsis of the Evaluative Study (Item *d* above)

This synopsis is not intended to be a critical review, but a reporting of one procedure utilized by the Topeka School System in its examination of the FLEX program. The study was not a controlled one; its design appeared to fit the Campbell and Stanley Pre-Experimental Design No. 2: "The One-Group Pre-test-Post-test Design" (Campbell and Stanley, 1963, p. 7).

During the pilot stage of the FLEX program, its designer attempted to determine whether it might bring about a significant change in foreign language aptitude.

The Pimsleur Language Aptitude Battery (Harcourt Brace Jovanovich) was administered as a pretest and post-test to 61 participants in the nine-month pilot course. The researcher had formulated the following null hypothesis—that there would be no significant change in foreign language aptitude upon the termination of the pilot course—and two subhypotheses—that there would be no significant change in verbal or auditory aptitude.

Differences between means in pretest and post-test were significant at the .05 level of confidence with respect to the *overall test, the auditory section,* and *the verbal section.*

A prequestionnaire and postquestionnaire were also administered to determine changes in attitude. During a telephone conversation, the researcher stated that the postquestionnaire had indicated a significant shift in attitude in the direction of positive feelings about foreign language study.

As a result of this investigation, the Topeka Schools concluded that there was a significant difference in foreign language aptitude upon completion of a nine-month FLEX course. The researcher generalized that an individual's aptitude for learning a foreign language could be improved by becoming acquainted with the foreign language field in general before choosing a language to study extensively.

The investigator also stated that further research on this topic, perhaps a controlled study, might be conducted in the Topeka Schools in the future.

Stratford Public Schools

This program was discontinued as described herein. However, a sixth-grade pilot program has been established, which contains similar components.

Detailed descriptions of the Stratford (Connecticut) program were obtained from the following sources:

- *Northeast Conference Reports* (Born, 1975, p. 94)
- *Foreign Language Annals* (Bourque, 1976, pp. 10-16)
- Indiana University Course on Exploratory Programs (Summer 1976)
- Personal interview with course designer
- Curriculum materials from the foreign language office of the Stratford Schools

According to school system documents, students in grade seven were introduced to foreign languages through a required exploratory course dealing with languages in general. Examples were drawn from various languages in order to illustrate differences and to provide a better understanding of English structure and vocabulary. The course was culture oriented, so that students learned about people of other countries and about their own ethnic backgrounds.

Course title: Exploratory Language and Culture

Year established: 1974-1975

Grade level: Seventh

Course duration: One year

Course type: General Language and Culture

Languages: Exposure to as many as possible (at least five)

Main goals: As stated in system document and in Bourque (1976, p. 11):

1. To develop appreciation for language and cultural differences
2. To stimulate interest in further language study.

General course objectives:

1. Motivation for language study
2. Mastery of a limited amount of language material

3. Improved study techniques, especially those useful in learning a language

4. Improved reading skills through vocabulary awareness and acquisition

5. Increased sensitivity to and appreciation of different cultures; decreased ethnocentrism

6. Better pupil placement in an eighth-grade beginning language course

7. An improved foreign language program with greater strength at the beginning and reduced attrition.

Specific student objectives: As stated by the school system:

The student will:

1. Be able to count to ten in several different foreign languages

2. Recite from memory, and with understanding, a brief dialogue in several different languages

3. Identify elementary differences between American and other cultures

4. Do independent research on cultural areas of particular interest

5. Do personal research on his or her own ethnic background and on the origin of his or her own name

6. Keep notes on and ask questions about cultural and linguistic facts presented by the teacher and by numerous guest speakers.

Materials used:

1. Locally prepared units

2. Commercially prepared materials, including audiovisual supplements

3. Realia

4. Community resources, including representatives of various cultures

Methodology:

1. Pupil-centered activities

2. Project-oriented activities

3. Community persons used as teacher-presenters.

Implementation, including type of content: No two exploratory courses were alike (Bourque, 1976, p. 12). All teachers involved were aware of course goals and student performance objectives. Classes were free to explore the languages reflected in the ethnic composition of members. However, all classes covered the following units: communication theories and the birth of language; kinesics, nonverbal communication; the alphabet; students' names and family heritage (voluntary in each class); languages of the world, including a brief history of English; American dialects; community awareness; the world community.

Organization: Each exploratory class was self-contained. All teachers taught only in their own school. This was unlike Topeka which utilized itinerant teachers. With the help of community resources, teachers included languages they did not know themselves.

Evaluation: According to school system document, evaluation consisted of:

1. Aural and oral testing of language

2. Written tests of language and culture

3. Reports, research papers, and projects.

Rochester Public Schools

Descriptive documents were obtained from the Rochester (New York) School District, from the previously noted Indiana University course in exploratory programs, and from discussion with the coordinator.

Course title: Person to Person—Linguistics Curriculum for Grade 7

Year established: 1973-1974

Grade level: Seventh

Course duration: One-third year (12 weeks)

Course type: General Language: A Linguistic Introduction to the Study of Language

Languages: Latin, Italian, French, Spanish, and German

Main goals: As given in the curriculum guide:

1. To provide a linguistic introduction to the study of language
2. To assist students to express ideas more effectively in speech and writing
3. To lead students to experience communication with different cultures.

Student performance objectives:

The student will:

1. Acquire a basic knowledge of the facts about language
2. Become aware of his or her own language and its relationship to other languages
3. Develop an understanding of the cultural and behavioral attitudes of the inhabitants of other countries
4. Develop an appreciation of other cultures
5. Become familiar with the languages taught in the district, and thus make a more knowledgeable choice
6. Develop a curiosity and interest in language.

Materials used:

1. Locally developed units
2. Text: *General Language*, Holt, Rinehart, and Winston, 1968
3. Specifically referenced sources in each unit, print and nonprint.

Methodology:

1. Teacher-directed class activities
2. Student projects.

Implementation, including type of content: Emphasis was on linguistic aspects. Each teacher was to cover curriculum as specified in the guide. The following units were the mainstay of the course: What Is Language?; Sign, Symbol, and Gesture; Language Acquisition and Development; The Dictionary; Onomastics; Writing Systems; History of Language; English and Its Dialects; Lessons *about* Latin, Italian, Spanish, French, and German.

Note: Learning of actual language samples was not a part of this course.

Organization: The exploratory linguistics curriculum was to be taught citywide to all seventh graders. The course was taught in each school by the foreign language staff of that school.

Evaluation: In addition to the usual recall-test procedures, no mention was made of evaluation in the curriculum documents submitted by the school system.

Baltimore County Public Schools

Information was gathered through personal discussions with supervisors of foreign languages and obtained from materials prepared by the Baltimore County, Maryland, school system.

Course title: Foreign Language Appreciation

Year established: 1970-1971

Grade level: Mostly seventh and some eighth

Course duration: One year (two or three times per week)

Course type: Language potpourri

Languages: French and Spanish (most schools). Some schools may include German, Russian, Hebrew, Chinese, or Italian, staff permitting.

Main goals: Summarized from the supervisor's response to questionnaire.

1. To broaden and enrich students' experiences through initial contact with other languages and cultures
2. To make students aware of processes of communication and language learning
3. To help students communicate a limited number of ideas through a new language system
4. To develop students' desire to extend foreign language study.

Course Objectives: Although objectives are not stated in performance terms, each unit includes student performance criteria.

1. To help students develop good listening habits for comprehension
2. To provide for students, experiences typical of youth of the target cultures, utilizing multiphased activities and experiences

3. To foster correct pronunciation within a limited framework of meaningful utterances in the foreign language explored

4. To provide limited reading and writing (copying) exercises to reinforce spoken forms.

Materials used:

1. Locally developed units, called "Experiences"

2. Multisensory materials.

Methodology:

1. Student-centered

2. Activity- and project-oriented.

Implementation, including type of content: Class sessions were held two or three times per week, unlike other courses described herein which were held daily. Course content was divided into a series of "Experiences" for each language explored. The components of each "Experience" were: objectives, conversational frames, cultural insights, songs and games, filmstrips and/or films, and student projects. Sample "Experiences": *Who Are You and How Are You?; Where Do You Live?*

Organization: The exploratory course was offered to all seventh graders and was generally taught by the foreign language staff of each school. Other interested teachers who knew a foreign language were utilized. The sequential program began in grade eight.

Evaluation: Student progress was evaluated in terms of desirable work habits, attitudes, and interest and participation in class activities.

No mention was made in the curricular documents of evaluation of the course itself.

Fairfax County Public Schools

Information was obtained from documents submitted by the Fairfax County (Virginia) school system, and through conversations with the supervisor of foreign languages.

Course title: Introduction to Foreign Language

Year established: 1974

Grade level: Seventh and eighth grades. It was also implemented for one year at the ninth-grade level.

Course duration: One semester

Course type: Language Potpourri

Languages: French and Spanish generally, with German and Latin for a shorter period

Main goals:

1. To familiarize students with the idea of language as a skill and as a basic form of human communication

2. To make students aware of the differences in other cultures and to help them understand, appreciate, and respect those differences

3. To strengthen the students' English skills and to increase their interest in foreign language study.

Specific student objectives:

Linguistic objectives: Students will study why and how to study a foreign language; how the specific language developed; the sounds of the language with some major intonation and stress patterns.

Grammar: Students are introduced to some basic verb forms, both regular and irregular, and to the personal pronouns. The basic vocabulary includes question words, vocabulary dealing with school and classroom objects, clothing, numbers, etc. Basic expressions include greetings, emergency expressions, how to tell time, and expressions to be used while shopping and while at a restaurant. Also introduced is vocabulary dealing with occupations, days of the week, months, weather, rooms of the house, family members, and colors.

Cultural objectives: Students will study geography, travel information, family life, sports, food habits, etiquette, and the influence that the language and the people have had on America. Also studied very briefly are the art, music, and literature of each country; its history in brief; plus the names of its famous persons.

Materials used:

Introduction to Foreign Language: French—Student Booklet, 1981

Introduction to Foreign Language: German—Student Booklet, 1981

Introduction to Foreign Language: Spanish—Student Booklet, 1981.

(These booklets were prepared by Fairfax County foreign language teachers.)

Methodology:

Using a team approach, students are introduced to basic sounds and phrases of the two or more languages they will study. Emphasis is given to contrasting the languages among themselves and with English, and also on how Latin has influenced them. Much time is spent on culture. Students are encouraged to work on projects either individually or in small groups. Students take field trips to places of interest. Community resource persons speak and make presentations to the class. Festivals are held at the end of the course, with food and exhibits from the various countries representing the languages explored.

Implementation:

The course is listed and described in the student course brochure so that those interested may register during registration month. There are no prerequisites. While some students begin in French, others begin in Spanish. After nine weeks they change classes. If Latin and German are included, those students will begin with three weeks of Latin, followed by six weeks of French, six of Spanish, and terminating with three weeks of German.

Organization:

The classes are offered at the seventh- and eighth-grade levels after which students may take a regular Level I course in the language of their choice. They may also drop foreign language study for a year or two, or altogether.

Evaluation:

Students are given many quizzes and some major tests based on the content studied. Also evaluated are participation in class and work on specific projects assigned.

Monroe County Community Schools

Although the Monroe County (Indiana) program was discontinued in 1975 because of severe budget cuts,* it was included in this review because of its impact on early exploratory curricula of the new cycle. Initiated in 1972-1973, it was the topic of a formal presentation by Judith C. Morrow, one of its developers, at the 1973 Central States Conference on Foreign Language Education. Upon subsequent publication in the conference reports (Morrow, 1974, pp. 119-43), it became, together with the Topeka program, a resource for organizers of exploratory courses.

Course title: Language and Man

Year established: 1972-1973

Grade level: Sixth and seventh; some eighth

Course duration: One year

Course type: General language and language potpourri

Languages: French and Spanish; Latin and German where teachers available. (No formal materials were developed for Latin and German.)

Main goals:

1. To sensitize students to foreign languages and cultures
2. To provide a basis for choosing a language for formal study.

Student performance objectives: Objectives seemed to parallel those of the Topeka program. Content was oriented more prominently toward a general language course. The concept of dialects and the significance of gestures, sign language, and body language in human communication were emphasized heavily. The investigation of one's own linguistic and cultural heritage was also an important component.

Evaluation: Procedures included testing students for achievement within the stated objectives. Program evaluation consisted of a questionnaire to pupils and an assessment of parental opinion.

---

*Information in written communication from the Director of Secondary Education, Monroe County Community School Corporation, Bloomington, Indiana.

Enrollment in regular language classes had been increasing as a result of this exploratory course. Morrow also referred to benefits accruing to the foreign language teachers who had been involved in the creation and implementation of this course. Among the benefits were the experiences of teaching languages to "all kinds of students," and the experience of designing new curriculum materials (p. 143).

Prince George's County Public Schools

Course title: Foreign Language Exploratory

Year established: 1973-1974

Grade level: Seventh, some eighth

Course duration: Junior high model: one year; middle school model: one semester

Course type: General language and language potpourri

Languages: French and Spanish; German, where possible; Latin and Greek—roots and affixes. Other languages were informally explored based on teacher background or community resources.

Main goals: As stated in school system documents (Prince George's County, Maryland, 1975, pp. 8-9):

1. To acquaint pupils with several languages for informed choice; for general education
2. To build readiness for future language study:
   a. linguistic principles
   b. awareness of structure
   c. language learning process in a less rigorous environment
   d. foreign language study habits, e.g., memorization, listening, copying
3. To expand pupils' English vocabulary through awareness of foreign elements and of the nature and history of language

4. To introduce pupils to foreign cultures—similarities and contrasts with the United States, and the contribution of these cultures to our nation

5. To reinforce career awareness concepts: foreign languages and the world of work

6. To foster positive pupil attitudes toward cultural and linguistic differences.

Notes: The goals of the exploratory program helped to achieve the following county goals for the junior high school:

1. To explore present interests and develop new ones

2. To investigate new areas and interests which may be related to future educational and occupational careers

3. To increase understanding of themselves and others (*Educational Master Plan, 1975,* p. V-B1).

Student end-of-course performance objectives:

1. **Linguistic skills—specific to the foreign languages explored**

   a. To *say* with understanding a specifically designated group of utterances taught for active control

   b. To *understand* these utterances when *heard* or *seen*

   c. To *understand* when *heard* or *seen*: a wider group of expressions taught for recognition only; *reading* recognition only: (without aural comprehension) road signs, posters, public signs, geographic names

   d. To *write,* in the form of copying foreign samples accurately; to spell accurately names of persons and places taught.

2. **General language skills and concepts ("English Connections")**

   a. To *relate* each language explored to English

   b. To *give meaning* of some of the most common Latin and Greek roots and affixes in English words

   c. To *discuss,* within their level of sophistication, history of language; language families

   d. To *recognize* some common foreign words and phrases used in English

   e. To *recognize* some basic differences among languages explored.

3. Pre-Level I skills and concepts

   a. To *demonstrate* understanding of: language as system of sounds; form and function in language; positional, inflectional, and intonational influence on meaning

   b. To *demonstrate* awareness of foreign language learning tasks: memorizing, copying, imitating, and repeating.

4. Cultural objectives

   a. To *demonstrate* awareness of contrasts and similarities among the different foreign cultures explored as well as between each foreign culture and the United States, to the extent that this information was part of the course

   b. To *demonstrate* a knowledge of the geography, historical highlights, social customs, and the world of work of the peoples whose languages were explored; their contribution to the development of the United States, to the extent taught

Note: The teacher predetermined with the class the degree of expectation with regard to items a and b, based on the specific content studied. Pupils were held responsible only for material previously agreed upon as meriting their active retention.

   c. To *reflect* an attitude of appreciation toward foreign cultures, as expressed in class discussions, and in behavior toward classmates and adults from other cultures.

5. Career awareness objectives

   a. To *examine* at least one of the 15 occupational clusters (Hoyt, 1974, pp. 31-32) as it related to one of the languages explored

   b. To *submit* a project demonstrating the above relationship

   c. To *acquire* some knowledge of possible relationships of foreign language skills to a variety of occupations, *demonstrated* through discussion and tests

   d. To *raise the level of decision-making skills* through exploration of a new discipline, with possible future career implications.

Materials used:

1. *General Language* (Holt, Rinehart and Winston—reprinted by permission). One copy for each student.

2. Print and nonprint: In addition to the *General Language* text, many books, pamphlets, maps, filmstrips, and other enrichment materials were utilized. (The basic set of materials used in the Prince George's County exploratory program are listed in chapter 6 of this book.)

Methodology:

1. Student-centered

2. Activity- and project-oriented

3. Teacher-centered for daily teaching of foreign language sample and general language content.

Implementation, including type of content: Class sessions were conducted in English except for foreign language segment. Classes met daily for both the year-long course in junior high school and the semester course in middle school. Course content was organized under the themes of language, culture, and career development.

1. **Language:**

    a. *General language:* Communication, language families, English dictionary skills and vocabulary building with Latin and Greek roots and affixes

    b. *Specific languages:* Required exploration of French and Spanish; optional exploration of German. Others according to interest

    c. *Foreign phrases and expressions* to say and/or recognize were grouped around categories such as "Making Friends," "Travel," "Shopping," etc., in the form of teaching units

    d. *English connections:* The relationship of the language explored to English; comparison with one another

    e. *Pre-Level I concepts:* Awareness of syntax, gender, agreement, building readiness for foreign language study.

2. **Culture:**

    a. *Formal and Deep Culture* (Brooks, 1966, p. 4; Valette, 1972, pp. 199-206)

    b. *World Areas in Focus for French:* France, Canada, Caribbean, West Africa, and Switzerland

For Spanish: Spain, Mexico, and Puerto Rico (Central and South America for special projects)

For German: West Germany, Austria, and Switzerland

c. *Sample cultural units:* "Peoples and Places," "Foods and Cooking," "Holidays and Festivals," "Family Names," in connection with language categories. (See *Language*.)

3. **Career Development:**

a. Foreign languages and the world of work

b. Decision-making skills (Beusch and De Lorenzo, 1977, pp. 9-17).

Organization: The following organizational models were used for the year's course.

1. **Model I:** French/Spanish—formal exploration

a. Two classes scheduled parallel

b. Two teachers—one French, one Spanish

c. Classes exchange teachers at the end of the first semester

d. Each class will have explored both languages at the end of year.

2. **Model II:** French, Spanish, and German—formal exploration

a. Two classes scheduled parallel

b. Two teachers—one French/Spanish (teacher A), one German/Spanish or German/French (teacher B)

c. Course divided into three 12-week segments

d. Teachers plan the exchange of classes so that a new language is introduced every 12 weeks

e. Each class will have explored all three languages by the end of the year.

3. **Model III:**
One class with one teacher who is competent in more than one foreign language, such as French-German, French-Spanish, or Spanish-German. Several such classes can be scheduled during the school day.

[**Note:** All models were to incorporate the study of how Latin and Greek have contributed to English, the most common roots and affixes; theories of language origins; the development of graphic symbols, and types of nonverbal communication.

All models could include a brief exposure to other languages taught in the Prince George's system, viz., Italian and Russian; and others of interest.

Last segment of course included linguistic comparisions.

Recommended maximum class enrollment: *28*

(Fryer, 1975, p. 29; Prince George's County, 1975, pp. 6-7).]

4. **Middle School Model:** The course can be taught by one teacher who knows at least French and Spanish. The content is telescoped into a semester format (Prince George's County, 1980, pp. 5-8).

Evaluation:

1. Pupil performance in relation to stated objectives (cognitive, affective, psychomotor)

2. Pretests and post-tests on linguistic and cultural concepts

3. An end-of-course survey test

4. Pupil opinion survey

5. Informal parent surveys

6. Monitoring by supervisory personnel

Pupils took a pretest on cultural and linguistic concepts. The teacher discussed the test with pupils afterward; tests were filed; and at the end of the course, pupils compared scores on the pretest with their performance on the post-test.

Speaking, listening, and reading recognition tests were given within the parameters of the course. Informal quizzes, which involved speaking skills, were administered several times per week through teacher-controlled conversation. In speaking, the criterion of comprehensibility was applied in lieu of Level I standards.

The testing of cultural material was based on the content of specific units taught and projects completed by pupils. Social Studies and English language-arts standards applied.

An end-of-course survey test was taken by all pupils in the Exploratory program.

Surveys of pupil attitudes and parental opinion were an integral part of the program.

Summary of Program Models

The foregoing programs are summarized in Figure 3-1. For a description of several more recently established exploratory programs see the 1983 *Northeast Conference Reports* (Omaggio, pp. 39, 51, 52).

Program	Course title	Year established	Type
Topeka, Kansas	Foreign Language Exploratory	1970-1971	General Language Language Potpourri
Baltimore County, Maryland	Foreign Language Appreciation	1970-1971	General Language Language Potpourri
Monroe County, Indiana	Language and Man	1972-1973 (elim. 1975)	General Language Language Potpourri
Rochester, New York	Person to Person	1973-1974	General Language
Prince George's County, Maryland	Foreign Language Exploratory	1973-1974	General Language Language Potpourri
Stratford, Connecticut	Exploratory Language and Culture	1974-1975 (modified)	General Language and Culture
Fairfax County, Virginia	Introduction to Foreign Languages	1974-1975	Language Potpourri

Figure 3-1. Summary chart of program models.

Chapter 4

Organizing the Exploratory Curriculum

This chapter presents a course model and procedures for designing an exploratory foreign language program. The main sources for the suggested model are the review of past and current programs, as reported in chapters 2 and 3, and results of a nationwide curriculum survey conducted by the authors. (A copy of the survey and detailed results are included in the Appendix.) The following summary provides a frame of reference for the model and procedures.

Survey for Curriculum Development

The authors submitted a survey questionnaire to state departments of education, selected school systems, and individual schools known to have exploratory programs. The purpose of the questionnaire was to determine trends in exploratory courses in type of course (format), unifying concepts, goals, and performance objectives. Highlights of the results are discussed here.

Type of Course

The course formats described most frequently by the respondents to the survey were: (1) language potpourri and (2) the combination of language potpourri with general language.

Additionally, the stated goals and performance objectives of those classifying their course as language potpourri revealed that a general language component had been incorporated at various points in the instructional plan. The distinction between these two classifications becomes blurred in practice. A combination of the two provides a program of greater breadth, and thus is more desirable.

Unifying Concepts

The survey included an inventory of concepts in language, culture, and career awareness. Respondents were asked to indicate the level of emphasis assigned to these concepts in their programs.

Those concepts which were assigned *high* to *moderate* emphasis are listed in Figure 4-1. This list may represent, in the authors' view, an emergent consensus regarding the concepts to be addressed in middle school exploratory courses. Despite locale and preferences of individual communities and course planners, this consensus prevails.

Alexander and Williams have stressed the need for undergirding middle school exploratory experiences with structured concept development (1965, p. 219). The list in Figure 4-1 forms a nucleus for structure in a foreign-language based exploratory curriculum to which additional concepts may be added.

For example, although the following concepts were cited for relatively low emphasis in the survey, they are considered sufficiently important by some foreign language educators to be included in exploratory courses (*Northeast Conference Reports*, 1983, pp. 132-34).

Language
- Derivation
- Development of human language
- Roots, prefixes, suffixes
- Dictionaries
- Concept of dialect differences
- Animal sounds
- Ancient languages
- Artificial languages

Culture

- Geography
- Immigrants
- Performing arts (music/singing)
- Religious customs

Career awareness

- Work standards
- Concept of work
- Occupational clusters

	Language	Culture	Career Awareness
H	communication	greetings	
	words	names/titles	
I	concept of language	wariness of	
	sounds and meaning	stereotyping	
G	sound systems	family	
	cognate formation	foods: preparation/	
H	gestures	dining	
	borrowing between	cultural connotation:	
	languages	words, phrases,	
	word order	gestures	
	"accent"	culture contrasts	
	language families/	friendship	
	geography	culture in language	
	writing/alphabets	culture, meaning	
	word form	homes	
	relationships	ethnic heritage—	
	word order	U.S.A.	
	relationships	famous figures	
	signs/symbols	proprieties/	
M	gender	improprieties	
	development of	language in culture	
O	English	sports	
	agreement	roles of women	
D	word forms	humor	leisure
	melody	schools	foreign languages/work
E	pluralization	myths/legends	world
	inflection	roles of children	career/occupation
R	modification	roles of men	work across cultures
	science/art of	self-concept across	work values across
A	language study	cultures	cultures
		time across cultures	work roles across
T		empathy	cultures (including
E		holidays/festivals	ancient cultures)

(right margin vertical label: M O D E R A T E)

Figure 4-1. Concepts for exploratory courses recommended for high-to-moderate emphasis by majority of respondents in nationwide survey.

Goals and Performance Objectives

The main goals and objectives of exploratory programs as described by the majority of respondents are listed in Figure 4-2. They are organized in categories according to the content of the responses.

GOALS

Attitudes
- Motivation for language study
- Decision making
- Cultural sensitivity
- Appreciation of heritage

Skills
- Preparation for language study
- English skills—vocabulary
- Survival level skills—foreign language
- Study skills

Knowledge
- Communication concepts
- Culture facts
- Language facts
    Structure
    Families
    Development

OBJECTIVES (for students)

Pertaining to:
- speaking within strictly defined limits
- recognizing spoken and written words specifically taught
- identifying elementary differences between U.S. and other cultures
- demonstrating respect for other cultures
- discussing how other cultures contribute to U.S.
- demonstrating knowledge of:
    language growth, families, gestures, signs
- applying foreign language study skills
- recognizing English cognates, borrowed words, derivations
- choosing a language to study

Figure 4-2. Goals and objectives for exploratory courses cited by the majority of respondents in nationwide survey.

Suggested Course Model and Procedures

The procedural section, which includes the suggested curriculum model, comprises the remainder of this chapter. This recommended model is based on the language potpourri/general language combination format which the authors feel is more enriching educationally than either format alone.

Model:
The Integrated
Language Experience

Suggested Course Model
and Procedures
for designing
Exploratory Foreign Language Courses
in Middle/Junior High School

This section has been prepared as an aid to teachers, administrators, and supervisors in planning exploratory courses in foreign languages for middle and junior high schools. It incorporates a suggested curriculum model, as well as procedures for organizing and implementing the course. The title of the model is "Integrated Language Experience."

The information is presented in a succinct style and format in order to enhance its usefulness. An overview of the topics is given below for the reader's convenience.

> **Model designs**
> **Course implementation**
>> Definitions and elements of the course
>> Rationale
>> Goals
>> Student performance objectives
>> Organization and administration
>> Methods and teacher training
>> Evaluation
>> Materials and references

In order to achieve a total course perspective, it is suggested that the user read the entire contents of this section before proceeding with plans.

Guidelines for Organization

A school or school system desirous of establishing an exploratory foreign language course should define for itself what the term *exploratory* is to encompass. An exploratory phase of a foreign language curriculum can best be designed by focusing on the content, goals, and objectives as contrasted with the sequential program. The designers of such a course must be careful to avoid both the watered-down Level I and the superficial fun-and-games approaches to course planning and implementation. The National Council of State Supervisors of Foreign Languages is concerned that working formulas for exploratory programs be structured to suit the age of the middle or junior high school student and not be "purely informational and fact-stuffing" (Enwall, 1975, pp. 1-2). See references at the end of this chapter.

Model (Integrated Language Experience)

A suggested curriculum model is presented on the following pages. The parameters of the model are established through several schematic representations, together with subsequent elaboration of components.

This model is best implemented as a year-long course, although it may be adapted to the exigencies of middle and junior high school scheduling, and telescoped into a semester time frame. Further reduction in time span, however, would entail modification and some loss of integrity for this particular course model. In keeping with the authors' recommended format as an "Integrated Language Experience," the schematics reflect a blending of *general* and *specific* language content, with the inclusion of a strong cultural component.

Anatomy of a Foreign Language Exploratory Course
Middle/Junior High School

Rationale

Goals
Cognitive
Affective

Evaluation

Objectives
Cognitive
Skills
Knowledge
Affective
Attitude

Components in Implementation

General Language
History/language
  development
Signs, symbols, and codes
History of English
Exploring English/foreign
  cognates, roots
Foreign language study
  (How to)

Specific Languages
Language samplings
Social categories
Cultural contrasts/similarities
Contemporary/historical
Heritage
Application
Career awareness
World of work
Career clusters
Foreign languages and service

Design No. 1
Unifying Concepts

Each Language Explored
Each Language Category
e.g., Making Friends

Teach meaningful phrases

English—Infuse prefixes, suffixes, roots, foreign phrases, structural contrasts

How to study a foreign language (build readiness)

Develop language concepts

Teach related cultural units

Infuse: Role in America
　　　Develop cultural
　　　　concepts

Infuse: Community awareness
　　　Foreign visitors

Teach about:　Human language development
　　　　　　　Latin and Greek roots (English)—Roman
　　　　　　　　and Greek cultures
　　　　　　　Metric system

Develop:　Overall linguistic and cultural concepts
　　　　　Career awareness

(Usual modern language samplings: French, German, and Spanish; others may be substituted or included on a less formal basis.)

Design No. 2
Total Course Perspective

Foreign Language
Exploratory Overview

Human
Language   LANGUAGE EXPLORED (by
Development   categories, e.g., Making Friends)

FRENCH
SPANISH
GERMAN   **Teach:**   Meaningful phrases

                Infuse: How to study a foreign language
                              (build readiness)

                Develop: Language concepts

                Infuse: English prefixes, suffixes, roots, foreign
                              phrases, structural contrasts

Concurrent
Course Nucleus   **RELATED CULTURE EXPLORED**

                Infuse: Contrasts with U.S.
                              Role in America
                              (historical/contemporary)
                              Community awareness
                              Foreign visitors

                Develop: Cultural concepts

                CAREER AWARENESS CONCEPTS

                Examine: *Latin* and *Greek* (roots, suffixes,
                              prefixes, culture)

                Infuse: Metric system

                Examine: Other languages briefly, e.g., Italian

Elaboration of Model Components

Curriculum design typically calls for attention to the following fundamental elements: objectives, subject matter, evaluation, organization, and method. These elements are reflected in components of this model, listed below in the order in which they are addressed. The *definition* and *subject matter* of this type of exploratory course are considered first in this elaboration in order to establish at the outset the nature of the course. As a convenient reference, model components are explicated in a modified outline question/answer format.

List of Components of the Model

    I.   Exploratory—(definitions/elements)
    II. Rationale, Goals, Objectives
    III. Organization/Administration
    IV. Methods/Teacher Training
    V. Evaluation/Course Controls
    VI. Materials/References

I. Exploratory—Definitions/Elements

A. What Is an Exploratory Foreign Language Course?
(Junior high school/middle school context)

This course may incorporate elements of:

general language
awareness of different languages and dialects
tryout or sampling of some languages
cultural content
career awareness

Relationship to a sequential language program

pre-Level I and nonsequential or self-contained

Its unifying elements

concepts of language, culture, and career awareness

B. General Language—What Is It?

Language, speech—development
Communication
Sounds, signs, symbols, gestures, codes
    examples: words, musical symbols, Morse code, deaf alphabet, travel, signs, writing

C. Language Awareness

Informal exploration
    language families
    world languages
    artificial languages, e.g., Esperanto

Formal exploration
sampling or "tryout" of specific languages
English connections and contrasts: roots, prefixes, suffixes, derivatives, and
borrowed words

D. "Tryout" or Sampling—Which Languages?

Languages of the school or system program
specified body of survival and/or conversational material
speaking; reading recognition; copying
foreign language study skills
Time frame: number of weeks per language; e.g., six weeks per sample
Usual sampling languages: French, Spanish, German, Italian, Russian, Latin
(two or more)

E. Cultural Content—How Determined?

Cultures represented by languages sampled
links and contrasts with American heritage
deep and formal culture (See chart.)

	Examples
Way-of-life	names
(deep culture)	family members
	forms of address
	greetings
	daily living
	holidays/festivals
	meals
	social customs:
	weddings
	funerals
	etc.
Civilization	fine arts
(formal culture)	historical figures
	folk tales/literature
	geography and related facts
	great cities in that culture
	monuments
	sports world
	etc.

F. Career Awareness—Infused into Content

Dimension I
World of work:
in cultures of the languages sampled
occupations
attitudes

in American culture
foreign languages/careers
relatable occupations

Dimension II
Career development process:
enhancement and extension of elementary school concepts:
people are interdependent
work involves production of goods and services by people and for people
work values may differ from culture to culture
wide variety of occupations may be grouped around clusters
school related to work world

II. Rationale, Goals, and Objectives

A. Why Have an Exploratory Foreign Language Course in the Middle/Junior High School?

Lack of foreign language exposure* in elementary school as part of:

cultural experiences
linguistic experiences
career education

Need to build readiness for study of the discipline

about new sounds
about new structures
about new study skills
about new cultures

Reinforcement of English skills through awareness of:

foreign elements
word histories
spelling patterns

Exploration

leading to a more informed choice concerning sequential language study

B. What Are the Goals?

Not to provide a smorgasbord of brief encounters with several languages**

But to provide:

*The first and most basic function of foreign language study is to release the student from the charmed circle of the language and culture in which he has been confined since childhood. (*Bulletin,* Council for Basic Education; 22, 4 (December 1977): 9.)

**Nelson Brooks, "Retrospect and Prospect," *Northeast Conference Reports,* 1976, p. 167.

(Cognitive Psychomotor)

A *preview* of the nature of language, its natural history, and its critical importance in the development of man and his culture

Exposure to a number of foreign languages and cultures

Insights into English vocabulary and structure through linguistic comparisons and study skills

Opportunity to develop limited skills and concepts in several specified languages, also applicable in further study

(Cognitive and Affective)

Career-awareness activities and materials relating to foreign languages
    foreign languages in a variety of careers
    awareness of career choices
    world of work in our own and other societies
    work attitudes

Insights leading to:

positive attitudes toward other cultures
appreciation of American heritage
open-mindedness and curiosity about language
assessment of immediate interest in formal language study
intellectual and attitudinal readiness for possible future language study

C. What Are Realistic Student Performance Objectives?

General language

demonstrate:
    awareness of ideas about language origins
    awareness of the world's major languages
    knowledge of common Latin and Greek roots, prefixes, and suffixes
        occurring in English
    understanding *communication* process as involving sounds, gestures, or
        symbols

Specific languages and cultures

recognize by their printed appearance words of the languages formally explored (usually French, German, Spanish, and Latin)

speak with understanding phrases in the above languages which have been taught for active use (modern languages only)

understand when *heard* or *read* the meaning of phrases which have been taught for comprehension only

recognize the more common public signs of the foreign culture: road signs, posters, commercial establishments, etc.

copy accurately words of the sampling languages, spelling correctly from memory names of foreign persons and places taught

apply the foreign language study skills of memorizing and listening *state* the meaning of common English words *borrowed from* or *related to* the explored languages

    demonstrate knowledge and appreciation of the geography, historical highlights, and social customs of the peoples representing the sampling languages, and their contribution to the American heritage

Career awareness

    show how foreign languages are part of the work world and specific occupations

    discuss the relationship and interdependence of workers

III. Organization and Administration

A. Organization

What Is the Optimal Sequence for the Stated Scope of the Course?*
(For *Scope* see I and II.)

    determine which modern languages and cultures are to be formally explored, e.g., French, Spanish, German, etc.

    teacher availability factor

    divide pupils' exploratory year into segments: semesters or four to six weeks

Time segment one

Concurrent {
general language introduction
language/culture (1)—develop limited skills
infuse Latin and Greek linguistic elements and cultures
career awareness
individual exploration of language of interest (optional)

Time segment two

Concurrent {
continued infusion of general language
language/culture (2)—develop limited skills
continued infusion of Latin and Greek linguistic elements and cultures
career awareness
individual exploration of language of interest (optional)

Time segment three

similar to above format
language/culture, etc. (3)

Recapitulation between segments

brief exposure to additional languages

teacher and community resources
pupil interest

comparisons among languages

---

*For a discussion of scope and sequence, see *Curriculum Theory* by George Beauchamp, Kagg Press, Wilmette, IL, 1975, p. 198. (Available through public library (inter-library loan) or from the publisher.)

[Note: All Exploratory teachers in a school should plan the program together—a *team* plan.]

Evaluation (See item V of this section.)

How Should Community Involvement Be Fostered?

exploratory letter to parents from the teacher or principal at the beginning of the term or at the beginning of a new time segment

parents and others invited to be linguistic and cultural resources

B. Administration

What Are Suggested Scheduling Patterns for this Model?

(Differentiated Staffing)*

One teacher per class

teacher competent in more than one language

One class, two teachers

teacher is given another assignment when not teaching the Exploratory class

Two classes—parallel—two teachers

exchange classes for a semester or other time segment

Itinerant teachers

[Note: (1) scheduling should facilitate interdisciplinary contacts between teachers of Exploratory and social studies, art, and music; (2) supervision should strive to maintain consistency in content and instructional practices among all teachers of the course; and (3) piloting in one or two schools crucial.]

Parent Information before Pupil Registration?

Exploratory material to parents by school system or school principal (independent school)

Grade Levels

Middle/Junior High School - Grades 6, 7, 8

decision: elective or required
availability of Level I: grades 7, 8, 9
maximum class size: 30

*References: *Foreign Language Appreciation—Spanish: A Curriculum Publication of the Baltimore County Schools.* Towson, Maryland, 1978. pp. 2-15.

IV. Methods and Teacher Training

A. Methodology (process)

How Is the Course to Be Taught? *
(For goals and objectives see II, A-C.)

General language, cultural, and informational goals

English is the medium of instruction
teacher preplanning
pupil-centered with teacher-pupil planning

Specific language skills

teacher-directed for limited skill development
pupil activities for reinforcement

Components in support of pupil objectives
English language skills and knowledge
learning of cultural concepts and information
learning of concepts across languages and cultures
increasing career awareness
basic foreign language skills
language learning *process*—readiness for foreign
language study

Specific Samples follow

Sample 1: Foreign Language Exploratory Basic Lesson Format

I.   Practicing

15 minutes {
Words, phrases, building dialogue
Speaking, reading, copying
Presentation of short dialogue by pupils
The English connection (must not be omitted)

Foreign Language Exploratory—Resource Guide and Handbook. Prince George's County Schools.
Upper Marlboro, Maryland, 1975. pp. 104-111.

II.   In-between part of period

25-30 minutes
$\left\{\begin{array}{l}\text{Work on: projects} \\ \text{Give: reports, dramatizations} \\ \text{Reading lesson: text, } \textit{General Language} \text{ or equivalent} \\ \text{Class discussion: teacher or student led; panel} \\ \text{Outside speaker} \\ \text{"Contract" projects}\end{array}\right.$

III.   Set plans

5 minutes
$\left\{\begin{array}{l}\text{Evaluate work period: Ask students what has been} \\ \quad \text{accomplished} \\ \text{Quick review of phrases practiced earlier}\end{array}\right.$

DO NOT OMIT PART III!

From Prince George's County Public Schools, Upper Marlboro, Maryland (by permission).

Sample 2: Teaching Foreign Language Exploratory—Examples of Daily Activities Pupils May Be Engaged in

(Teachers must have a plan for specific activities each day.)

Planning Pyramid

1. Teacher should prepare the year's general plan for himself/herself.

2. From this, teacher plans by the week—gives pupils ditto with overall weekly plan on Fridays for the following week.

3. Weekly plan yields the daily tasks—end of week should involve a few minutes of evaluation with the pupils at which time teacher and pupils ask themselves: "How did we do?" Having a weekly plan does not mean that plan cannot be modified to meet a daily need for change.

From Prince George's County Public Schools, Upper Marlboro, Maryland (by permission).

Sample 3: Activities—"Hands-On"

(This list is not exhaustive.)

(Students perform the activities and make the materials, not the teacher. The teacher sets the stage, guides the proceedings, and insists on quality.)

Required of all pupils:

1. *Cultural or language project* for each language explored. (Investigating a country is a suitable project.)

2. *Career awareness project* for each language studied.

3. Keep a notebook for the course, which might include vocabulary, cultural information, and other materials of importance. Should be graded by teacher.

Things to Do and Make

Cultural Activities

Do:
- Team dialogues
- cultural skits
- recognition games, reports, panels, field trips/packets

Make:
- dioramas showing cultural aspects
- drawings with labels
- cultural and language book
- charts
- cooking activities
- tasting activities
- flour, salt, water maps
- menus
- schoolwide projects
- showcase displays
- cartoons
- metric materials—charts
- teaching aids (made by students), such as clocks
- puppets

Language Activities

- making flashcards for vocabulary/ structures
- crossword puzzles, some teacher-made, others student-made
- collages (using vocabulary and phrases)
- pairing-off—practicing the language
- posters *illustrating* words
- cognate charts
- matching phrases with pictures
- picture dictionary of foreign language vocabulary
- word recognition signs
- symbols charts
- learning deaf alphabet
- learning Morse code

From Prince George's County Public Schools, Upper Marlboro, Maryland (by permission).

Sample 4: Suggestions for Using a General Language Text in Exploratory Course

1. Use chapters on *history of language* during first segment

2. Teach material on *history of English* during first segment

3. *Chapter dealing with language being formally explored:*

   a. Infuse parts as class proceeds through the exploration

   b. Derive meaningful daily lessons from small portions—e.g., prepare worksheets which pupils execute through reading the text.

4. *Directed reading lesson from text*

   a. Decide which part of chapter

   b. Build *readiness:*

      1) Establish immediate reason for reading

      2) Explain new words or concepts—elicit pupil participation in "discovery" of meaning—use overhead projector if possible

      3) Ask a few questions to guide the reading

      4) Have students read silently a small segment at a time (determine empirically)

      5) Different students "read the part" that answers questions posed.

   c. Alternatives to no. 5 above

      1) Paragraphs assigned previous day to different pupils; they are to read their part aloud and explain it

      2) Students "read along" with text which has been taped

      3) Reading passages assigned to pupils previous day, with a variety of activities to prepare

      4) Pupils handed list of questions to which they must seek answers by reading the text

      5) Pupils are assigned dictionary work as follow-up: English words, borrowed foreign words, as related to the language being explored or to Latin and Greek

      6) In relation to item 5 above, use overhead projector in working with roots and affixes.

From Prince George's County Public Schools, Upper Marlboro, Maryland (by permission).

Sample 5: Foreign Language Exploratory— Schema for Each Language

(Broad Student-Centered Units with Teacher/Pupil Planning)

LANGUAGE

Practicing - teacher-led; student-led phrases
(Short dialogues - limited drills)

LANGUAGE - CULTURE - CAREER DEVELOPMENT FOREIGN VISITOR/IMMIGRANT (Course Components)

Discussing (Teacher and student led)
Panel type

Reporting (oral and written)
  Small group
  Individual
  Dramatizations
  Simulations

Learning Centers

Learning Activity Packets

Contract

Group Work/Individual Work
  Projects

Field Trips

CULMINATION—each language explored

EVALUATION—each language explored
  Teacher-Student
  Student-Course
  Student-Self
  Parent-Course

Review of outcomes vis-à-vis objectives

From *Foreign Language Exploratory,* Prince George's County Public Schools, Upper Marlboro, Maryland, 1975, p. 104. (By permission.)

Sample 6-a: Cultural Insights

Teach the following directed reading lesson:

I.   Topic: French Place Names in the United States

II. Objectives
     A. To make the students aware of French influences in the United States

     B. To identify and label on a map various American cities whose names
        are of French origin

III. Material
     A. Reading: French Place Names in the United States

     B. Dittoed map of the United States

     C. Transparency of map of the United States

IV. Procedure
     A. Teacher asks questions:
        1. Do you know of any towns or cities in Maryland or anywhere in the
           United States which bear French names?

        2. Do you know of any famous French people who had a great influence
           in America?

     B. Pass out the reading and list of cities with French names, found on pages
        339-340, pointing out the differences between the American and French
        pronunciations. (Facsimiles of pages 339 and 340 follow.)

     C. Students read and the teacher discusses with the students the origin of the
        names of the cities.

V.   Follow-up
     A. Teacher passes out map of the United States on page 341. (See Sample
        6-b)
        1. Have the students identify the cities as located by the letters on the
           map. Give a prize for the most correct list.

Teacher's Key

A.	Bel Air	N.	Bayonne
B.	Havre de Grace	O.	Montclair
C.	Joliet	P.	New Rochelle
D.	Terre Haute	Q.	Fayetteville
E.	Louisville	R.	Macon
F.	Des Moines	S.	Bellefonte
G.	Baton Rouge	T.	Duquesne
H.	New Orleans	U.	Beaumont
I.	St. Louis	V.	Pierre
J.	Detroit	W.	Montpelier
K.	Sault Sainte Marie	X.	Chantilly
L.	Duluth	Y.	Eau Claire
M.	Butte	Z.	Racine

2. Elicit from the students their ideas as to why most of the names of French origin are located in the eastern United States.

B. Have the students examine a Baltimore street map to find names of French origin.

From *Foreign Language Appreciation—French,* Baltimore County Schools, Towson, Maryland, 1978, p. 338. (By permission.)

Sample 6-b: Experience Eight—Geography Cultural Insights

FRENCH PLACE NAMES IN THE UNITED STATES

There are thousands of places in America which have French names. These names bear witness to the tremendous role the French played in the discovery and founding of the United States. Names of French cities, historical figures, and explorers are scattered throughout this country.

Here in Maryland, we have Bel Air and Havre de Grace (Harford County), Dunkirk (Calvert County), and Doubs (Frederick County).

Listed below is a partial list of the more inportant places in other parts of the U.S.A. bearing names of French origin.

Joliet (Illinois)
New Orleans (Louisiana)
Baton Rouge (Louisiana)
Des Moines (Iowa)
Terre Haute (Indiana)
Bayonne (New Jersey)
Butte (Montana)
Montclair (New Jersey)
New Rochelle (New Jersey)
Fayetteville (North Carolina)
Macon (Georgia)
Bellefonte (Pennsylvania)
Duquesne (Pennsylvania)

St. Louis (Missouri)
Louisville (Kentucky)
Detroit (Michigan)
Sault Sainte Marie (Michigan)
Duluth (Minnesota)
Pierre (South Dakota)
Beaumont (Texas)
Paris (Texas, Virginia)
Montpelier (Vermont)
Chantilly (Virginia)
Eau Claire (Wisconsin)
Racine (Wisconsin)
Laramie (Wyoming)

From *Foreign Language Appreciation—French,* Baltimore County Schools, Towson, Maryland, 1978, p. 339. (By permission.)

Experience Eight—Geography
Cultural Insights

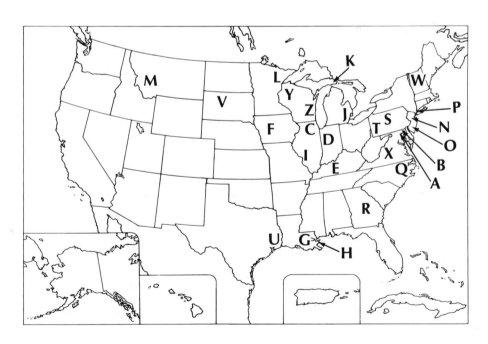

From *Foreign Language Appreciation—French,* Baltimore County Schools, Towson, Maryland, 1978, p. 341. (By permission.)

Sample 7: Experience Eight—Family Life

Vocabulary

¿Qué quiere ser?

	Spanish	English
Quiero ser	médico	_____
	doctor	_____
	actor	_____
	músico	_____
	artista	_____
	profesor	_____
	dentista	_____
	policía	_____
	secretaria	_____
	carpintero	_____

How can these people use a foreign language?

_____

_____

_____

_____

_____

From: *Foreign Language Appreciation—Spanish,* Baltimore County Schools, Towson, Maryland, 1978, p. 335. (By permission.)

Sample 8: German Exploratory

Sample Content: Recognition Questions to be
Answered in English

Wir machen eine Reise (trip) nach Deutschland!

Wir suchen Information über Westdeutschland.

Wo finden wir Information?

In der Klasse
In Buchern, in Magazine
Wir sehen Filme
Wir studieren in der Bibliothek.

Wir machen kleine Gruppen und lernen zusammen...	Welche Gruppe wollen Sie? Oder studieren Sie besser allein?
Eine Gruppe gibt Information über	Reise vorbereitungen (travel) preparations—German words are long!
	Das Klima
	Der Pass
	Das Visum
	Was kostet das?
	Flugzeug
	Frachter
	Dampfer?
	Transportation in Deutschland?
	Züge Restaurants
	Hotels Gasthäuser
	Jugendherbergen
	Das Geld - Dollar - Deutsche Mark

From *Foreign Language Exploratory*, Prince George's County Schools, Upper Marlboro, Maryland, 1975, p. 139. (By permission.)

B. Teacher Training

What is the Main Thrust of Teacher Training? (In-service and Preservice)

Exploratory foreign language teachers need

breadth:

for one-language major:

increasing knowledge about other languages
acquiring survival skills in second foreign language

for all foreign language Exploratory teachers:

improving knowledge of:

cultural details
overriding cultural and linguistic concepts
roots of English
other fields (e.g., music, art, social studies)
mathematics (metrics)
classical heritage
career education concepts

flexibility:

improved techniques for teaching content other than foreign language

activity-centered classroom
teacher-pupil planning
subgrouping and other forms of individualization
meeting broader range of needs

organizational skills:

planning multimedia course (print and nonprint)

implementing multidisciplinary facets
tentative individual or team plan before the beginning of the school
    year
utlilzing resources of other disciplines
planning for diverse pupil "hands-on" activities
follow-through

[Note: Student teachers assigned to schools with Exploratory programs.]

V. EVALUATION
A. Possible Course Controls

System Quality Control

curriculum guide
required teacher plan
course description/objectives to parents
end-of-year survey test (flexible model)
pupil opinion survey (See Sample 9.)
pretest on concepts
post-test on concepts

B. Survey Procedures

Feedback Concerning Course?

community/parents
pupils
teachers
administrators
supervisor-coordinator

C. Assessment

Are Pupils Meeting Stated Performance Objectives? (For *Objectives* see II, C.)

Evaluation

pupils-self
teacher-pupils:
   pupil feedback
   testing (see below)

Tests in the Exploratory Course

What Is to Be Tested?
words and phrases of the languages sampled
cultural details taught for retention (cognitive/affective)
general language facts
roots and affixes in English vocabulary (within the limits taught)
readiness aspect of foreign language learning, e.g., position of words in
   sentences
concepts of language and culture
career awareness concepts

Tests in the Exploratory Course

What Types of Tests?
(*Guiding Principle:* Test only what was taught and within the specific
   objective originally designated for each item.)

Teacher-made formal and informal tests (See Samples 10-12.)

   majority criterion-referenced
   some individualized or differentiated
   frequent quizzes; periodic term tests
   a systemwide end-of-year survey test*

Skills: Listening comprehension

   testing only the specific items taught
   no detailed listening comprehension tests
   tests for general recognition of differences between languages

Speaking
   utterances taught—test in situational context

Reading
   major subskill: recognition

*The separate sections of this test could be determined by a consensus of the teachers; the questions in each section could be chosen by individual teachers or departments.

Writing
    copying
    spelling (from memory)
        persons and places
        predetermined words from sampled language
        English vocabulary

Content
    only material agreed upon for retention (cognitive)
    attitudinal surveys and culture capsules (affective)

[Note: Use multiple choice, matching, essay, completion, and true/false tests. Also use realia, visuals, audiovisuals, and group competitions, as well as paper/pencil tests.]

D. Grading

Course
    standards similar to other courses in middle/junior high school for content phase
    pupils are evaluated according to the degree to which they achieve objectives

Special note on speaking skill

    Experience in Exploratory classes in a number of school systems has shown that the teacher must make a subjective judgment as to the acceptable level of pupil performance. The criterion of comprehensibility should apply for nonsequential courses rather than Level I standards.

Specific Samples follow

Sample 9: Pupil Opinion Survey

Dear Pupils of the Foreign Language Exploratory Course:

We need to know your opinion about the course. Please check your *agreement* or *disagreement* with the sentences given below by following the directions. There is no *right* or *wrong* answer, only your own opinion. We thank you for your help. DO NOT SIGN YOUR NAME.

Directions

If you <u>A</u>gree—mark   ✓/ / / /
                                       A SA U D SD

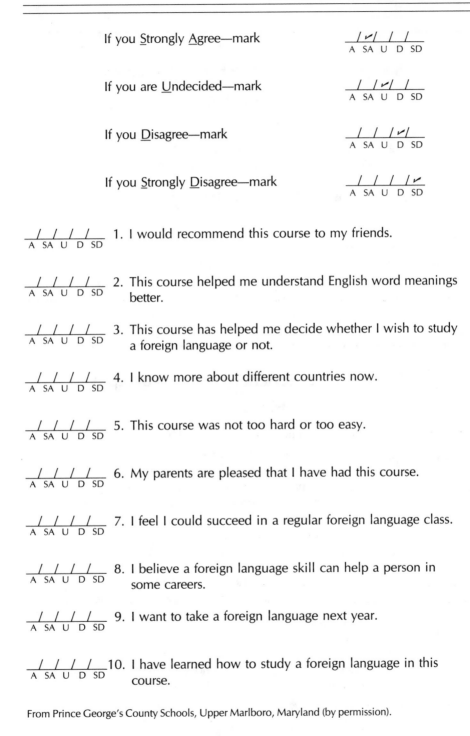

If you <u>S</u>trongly <u>A</u>gree—mark   / ✓/ / /
                                            A SA U D SD

If you are <u>U</u>ndecided—mark   / /✓/ /
                                            A SA U D SD

If you <u>D</u>isagree—mark   / / /✓/
                                            A SA U D SD

If you <u>S</u>trongly <u>D</u>isagree—mark / / / /✓
                                            A SA U D SD

/ / / / / 1. I would recommend this course to my friends.
A SA U D SD

/ / / / / 2. This course helped me understand English word meanings
A SA U D SD   better.

/ / / / / 3. This course has helped me decide whether I wish to study
A SA U D SD   a foreign language or not.

/ / / / / 4. I know more about different countries now.
A SA U D SD

/ / / / / 5. This course was not too hard or too easy.
A SA U D SD

/ / / / / 6. My parents are pleased that I have had this course.
A SA U D SD

/ / / / / 7. I feel I could succeed in a regular foreign language class.
A SA U D SD

/ / / / / 8. I believe a foreign language skill can help a person in
A SA U D SD   some careers.

/ / / / / 9. I want to take a foreign language next year.
A SA U D SD

/ / / / / 10. I have learned how to study a foreign language in this
A SA U D SD   course.

From Prince George's County Schools, Upper Marlboro, Maryland (by permission).

Sample 10: Experience Eight—Geography
Evaluation

Matching:

_____	1. la ville	A. the Rockies
_____	2. la montagne	B. the Atlantic
_____	3. la rivière	C. United States
_____	4. la province	D. east
_____	5. les Etats-Unis	E. Baltimore
_____	6. l'océan	F. the Mississippi
_____	7. le port	G. France
_____	8. le pays	H. Normandie
_____	9. est	I. south
_____	10. sud	J. Denver

From *Foreign Language Appreciation—French,* Baltimore County Public Schools, Towson, Maryland, 1978, p. 368. (By permission.)

Sample 11: Experience Eight—Geography
Evaluation

Match the definition with the French expression found below.

_____ 1. pie eaten with ice cream
_____ 2. an appointment; meeting place
_____ 3. a man or woman engaged to be married
_____ 4. the first performance of a movie
_____ 5. have a good trip
_____ 6. the cooking of a country
_____ 7. each item on menu is priced separately
_____ 8. appetizers
_____ 9. a person who knows fine food
_____10. main course of a meal (in the United States)

A. rendez-vous	F. première
B. cuisine	G. entrée
C. à la carte	H. à la mode
D. fiancé(e)	I. hors-d'œuvre
E. gourmet	J. bon voyage

From *Foreign Language Appreciation—French,* Baltimore County Public Schools, Towson, Maryland, 1978, p. 367. (By permission.)

Sample 12: Spanish Exploratory: Sample Test

Recall

Each student is called upon to give a reply to a certain question or questions.

NOTE: The phrases could be on the board, the teacher reads the description of the situation; the students choose the correct phrase.

1. You wish to ask for help.

2. How would you tell someone that you like to swim?

3. How would you ask someone his/her name?

4. If a Spanish-speaking person asks you *¿Qué hora es?* what would be your reply?

5. How would you say that you do not understand?

6. How would you say *I don't know?*

7. How would you ask *Where is the post office?*

8. How would you reply, *The post office is over there?*

a. ¿Dónde está el correo?

b. Son las _____. (Es la una.)

c. ¿Cómo se llama Ud.?

d. Allí está el correo.

e. No entiendo.

f. Me gusta nadar.

g. Yo no sé.

h. ¿Me puede ayudar?

From *Foreign Language Exploratory*, Prince George's County Public Schools, Upper Marlboro, Maryland, 1975, p. 169. (By permission.)

VI. Materials and References

A. Materials and Sources

Special notes:

(1) Schools or systems establishing an Exploratory program should be aware that some materials, both print and nonprint, which are part of the inventory of foreign language departments may be *adapted* to this type of course. Also, school media specialists should be consulted for lists of materials available in the media center or library, such as issues of *National Geographic Magazine*, filmstrips/slides, and for obtaining suitable films from system holdings. (Thus initial outlay of funds can be somewhat reduced.)

(2) This compilation emphasizes sources more than specific items. However, those items uniquely applicable to the course and not widely available are listed by both name and source.

(3) One of the characteristics of this course model is the *involvement of pupils in the creation of materials* which are used in class for teaching and learning, such as word posters, flashcards, charts, and dioramas. Hence administrators should consider the purchase of both the finished commercial product and materials which can be used for *creating* classroom aids.

1. School Systems

(Sources of program materials, guides, and sample instructional units)

These school systems have indicated a willingness to share materials:

Baltimore County Public Schools
Towson, Maryland 21204

Indianapolis Public Schools*
Indianapolis, Indiana 46204

Public Schools of Topeka
Topeka, Kansas 66612

Prince George's County Public Schools
Upper Marlboro, Maryland 20772

Stratford Public Schools
Stratford, Connecticut 06430

2. General Language Concepts and Specific Languages (for sampling)

American Classical League Service Bureau
Miami University
Oxford, Ohio 45056
(Latin and Greek elements in English—charts, etc.)

French for Travelers
(also German, Italian, Russian, and Spanish)
Macmillan Publishing Company
Front and Brown Streets
Riverside, New Jersey 08075

General Language: English and Its Foreign Relations
Lilly Lindquist and Clarence Wachner
Holt, Rinehart, and Winston (1968)
383 Madison Avenue
New York, New York 10017

---

*Resource for developing English skills through foreign elements: *Augmenting Reading Skills through Language Learning Transfer* (1978 publication).

[Note: Though out of print, the firm will grant school systems permission to reproduce, *on written request*. The only available general language text.]

J. Weston Walch
Box 658
Portland, Maine 04104
(*History of Language* posters)

Speaking of Language (filmstrip/cassette)
Guidance Associates
Communications Park
Mt. Kisco, New York 10549

Passport to French
(also German, Spanish)
World Publishing Company
2080 West - 117th Street
Cleveland, Ohio 44111

3. **Cultural Concepts and Information**

American Council on the Teaching of Foreign Languages
579 Broadway
Hastings-on-Hudson, New York 10706
Materials Center
(*Publications* on cultural projects, career awareness; items specific for Exploratory courses.)

American Language Teacher
Box 07300
Detroit, Michigan 48207
(*French, German, Spanish Teenager*)

Newbury House Publishers
Rowley, Massachusetts 01969
(*Culture capsules on various countries*)

David C. Cook
School Products Division
Elgin, Illinois 60120
(*Metric system charts*)

David McKay Company
750 Third Avenue
New York, New York 10018
(*Travel and culture guides*)

Rand McNally and Company
P.O. Box 7600
Chicago, Illinois 60680
(Wall map: Languages of the World and wall maps of countries—foreign text.)

EMC Corporation
180 East Sixth Street
St. Paul, Minnesota 55101
(Cultural filmstrips/discs/cassettes and career education materials.)

Gessler Publishing Company
220 East 23rd Street
New York, New York 10010
(Realia, songs, and audiovisuals.)

Harcourt, Brace, Jovanovich
5 Sampson Street
Saddle Brook, New Jersey 07662
(SO IST ES—German cultural, pictorial reader.)

J. Weston Walch
Box 658
Portland, Maine 04104
(Basic French Gestures and *Basic Spanish Gestures)*

Learning Arts
P.O. Box 917
Wichita, Kansas 67201
(Caribbean area filmstrips.)

Pathescope Industrial Media
71 Weyman Avenue
New Rochelle, New York 10802
(Cultural filmstrips: France, Germany, Mexico, ancient Rome, and Greece.)

Scholastic Foreign Language Services
902 Sylvan Avenue
Englewood Cliffs, New Jersey 07632
(Student newspapers in French, Spanish, and German.)

Scott, Foresman and Company
1900 East Lake Avenue
Glenview, Illinois 60025
(People of the World Series—texts: Mexico, France, and Germany.)

Silver Burdett Company
Morristown, New Jersey 07960
(*Hispanic American Music and Its Roots*—disc/booklet; texts on countries and
    cultures; and *Living in Puerto Rico*—posters and manual.)

Spanish Heritage Association
115-10 Queens Boulevard
Forest Hills, New York 11375
(Slides on Spain.)

Wible Language Institute
24 South Eighth Street
Allentown, Pennsylvania 18105
(Slides, filmstrips, vocabulary aids, etc.)

4. **Career Awareness Information and Materials**

American Association of Teachers of French
59 East Armory Avenue
Champaign, Illinois 61820
(Filmstrip/cassette—*Why Study French?*)

American Council on the Teaching of Foreign Languages
579 Broadway
Hastings-on-Hudson, New York 10706
Materials Center Publications

Columbia Language Services
P.O. Box 28365
Washington, D.C. 20005
(*Foreign Languages and Your Career*—Bourgoin.)

Curriculum Innovations, Inc.
Highwood, Illinois 60040
(*Career World*—a monthly magazine addressed to students, with teacher
    planning section.)

EMC Corporation
180 East Sixth Street
St. Paul, Minnesota 55101
(*Audiovisual materials on careers.*)

Houghton Mifflin Publishers
One Beacon Street
Boston, Massachusetts 02107
(*Career Opportunities Box for Foreign Languages*—filmstrip/cassette also
    available.)

National Textbook Company
4255 West Touhy Avenue
Lincolnwood, Illinois 60646
(*Foreign Language Careers,* Huebener.)

New York State Association of Foreign Language Teachers
1102 Ardsley Road
Schenectady, New York 12308
(Filmstrip/cassette—*Why Study Foreign Languages?* Publication—*Foreign Languages in Careers.*)

Regents Publishing Company
2 Park Avenue
New York, New York 10016
(*Careers in Foreign Languages,* Sherif.)

[Note: Schools may obtain (usually free of charge) brochures and other materials for students from such firms as airlines, food companies, etc. Branches of the federal government send brochures on careers.]

B. **References—Professional**

[Note: Write school systems listed under Materials, part A, for samples of curriculum planning and units.]

Adcock, Dwayne. "Foreign Languages in Elementary and Emerging Adolescent Education," in *ACTFL Review of Foreign Language Education,* vol. 8, Lincolnwood, IL: National Textbook Co., 1976, pp. 289-325.

Beauchamp, George A. *Curriculum Theory.* Wilmette, IL: The Kagg Press, 1975, pp. 198-99.

Bloom, Benjamin, and Krathwohl, David. *Taxonomy of Educational Objectives.* New York: David McKay Company, 1956. Handbook I, *Cognitive;* Handbook II, *Affective.*

Bourque, Jane, and Chehy, Linda. "Exploratory Language and Culture: A Unique Program," *Foreign Language Annals,* 9 (February 1976): 10-16.

Brannon, R. Marshall, and Cox, David E. "Coping with Real Problems in the Secondary School," in *ACTFL Review of Foreign Language Education,* vol. 8, Lincolnwood, IL: National Textbook Co., 1976, pp. 169-70.

Enwall, Beverly. *Position paper of National Council of State Supervisors of Foreign Languages.* New York: American Council on the Teaching of Foreign Languages, 1975.

Fryer, Bruce, "Free to Explore: Curricular Developments," in *ACTFL Review of Foreign Language Education,* vol. 7, Lincolnwood, IL: National Textbook Co., 1975, pp. 26-29.

Grittner, Frank M. "Foreign Languages and the Changing Curriculum," *Bulletin of the Association of Secondary School Principals,* (October 1974): 71-78.

Hoyt, Kenneth B.; Pinson, Nancy M; et al., editors. *Career Education and the Elementary School Teacher.* Salt Lake City: Olympus Publishing Company, 1973.

Karlin, Muriel Schoenbrun, editor. *The Career Education Workshop.* West Nyack, NY: Parker Publishing Company. (Monthly periodical.)

Kroll, Arthur M.; Dinklage, Lillian B.; et al. *Career Development—Growth and Crisis.* New York: John Wiley and Sons, 1970.

Mangum, Garth L.; Becker, James W.; et al., editors. *Career Education in the Academic Classroom.* Salt Lake City: Olympus Publishing Company, 1975. (See Chapter 7.)

Morrow, Judith C. "Exploratory Courses for the Middle and Junior High School," in *Student Motivation and the Foreign Language Teacher.* Frank Grittner, editor. Lincolnwood, IL: National Textbook Co., 1974, pp. 119-43.

Nostrand, Howard L. "Empathy for a Second Culture: Motivations and Techniques," in *ACTFL Review of Foreign Language Education,* vol. 5, Lincolnwood, IL: National Textbook Co., 1974, pp. 263-327.

Seelye, H. Ned. *Teaching Culture.* Lincolnwood, IL: National Textbook Co., 1984.

Taba, Hilda. *Curriculum Development—Theory and Practice.* Orlando, Florida: Harcourt, Brace, Jovanovich, 1962, pp. 425-26.

Chapter 5

Preparation of the Exploratory Teacher

In addition to a rationale and a theoretical basis for exploratory courses, the foregoing chapters of this book offer suggestions for their organization and content. The entire text may serve as a teacher training tool. Therefore, the authors included an outline and discussion of some approaches to the preparation of preservice and in-service teachers for conducting exploratory courses at both the pre-college/university and post-secondary levels.

The procedures section in chapter 4 lists several teacher qualities that are indispensable to implementing an exploratory course. Among the most essential qualities are breadth of linguistic and cultural knowledge and skill in organizing materials for instruction, as well as skill in utilizing a variety of grouping techniques and classroom activities. The authors conducted a nationwide survey which revealed that English teachers, as well as foreign language teachers, were involved in teaching exploratory courses. Since the Integrated Language Experience Model advocated in this book requires that a foreign language teacher teach the course, it is considered part of the foreign language program. Therefore, the exploratory teacher should be a foreign language major with a specialization in two languages or at least some familiarity with a second or third foreign language. Although the survival skill level in a second or third foreign language may be considered linguistically adequate for teaching an exploratory course,[1] knowledge of the culture should be more extensive.

This chapter focuses on the content and methods in the professional education of current and potential teachers of exploratory courses. Specifically, it presents suggestions for: (1) exploratory-oriented content courses at the post-secondary level; (2) an exploratory methods course; and (3) in-service training for exploratory teachers.

---

[1]Experience in the Prince George's County, Maryland, schools has shown that foreign language majors teaching the exploratory course have had little difficulty acquiring survival skills in another language when it has been necessary.

Exploratory-Oriented Content Courses at the Post-Secondary Level

All general college-level courses have the potential of contributing to the teacher's knowledge. However, a *general language course* would provide a comprehensive background for the prospective exploratory teacher. Courses of this nature, though still rare, do exist, and are being reestablished in increasing numbers after a thirty- to forty-year hiatus.[2] They are sometimes recognizable under titles like "World of Language," "Cultural Introduction to Foreign Languages," and "General Language."

Two existing models which demonstrate the type of content usually presented in college-level general language courses are described below.

The Murray State Model

In 1972, Keller and Ferguson (1976, pp. 50-55) developed a general language course at Murray State University in Murray, Kentucky. The course, "A Cultural Introduction to Foreign Languages," is available to the general student population as well as to language majors and minors as a three-hour credit elective in the humanities area.

The stated aims of the course are to emphasize the nature and importance of languages, to orient students to language study, and to help language majors and minors to expand their knowledge of communication and cultures. An outcome of the course is the students' greater awareness of the interrelationships among various disciplines, e.g., anthropology, philosophy, and psychology, as well as languages and linguistics.

The course is conducted as an interdisciplinary endeavor. One professor serves as coordinator and teaches approximately fifty percent of the classes. This instructor is also present at all lectures and is responsible for course planning and examinations. Instructors from each of the four languages taught at the university, as well as lecturers from other departments, contribute to the course. This arrangement has promoted reciprocity and increased dialogue among these departments.

The following are nine components of the course content.

---

[2]The May 1944 issue of the *Modern Language Journal,* for example, included an article by Siegfried Müller in which he set forth suggested content for a college course to help train secondary school teachers to teach in an exploratory program: "The General Language Course in the College Curriculum," pp. 425-29. The content proposed was surprisingly similar to that of contemporary courses.

"A Cultural Introduction to Foreign Languages"

(1) The land and the effects of geography on language; expansion of languages through colonization and migration; development of dialects in regions and in large cities; Black English.

(2) Origins of language and evolution of dialects into separate languages; translating; evolution of English and its place in the Indo-European family.

(3) Deep culture of language; effects of structure on thought; differing philosophical systems in relation to basic linguistic organization; sexist orientations of language.

(4) Structure in language as the element of order in communication; similarity of Germanic, Romance, and Slavic grammars; differences in Chinese and Japanese grammar and writing systems.

(5) Study of sample dialogues and drills in French, German, Russian, and Spanish.

(6) Language and science; a brief survey of scientific contributions from countries in which French, German, Russian, or Spanish is spoken; "international" words of science.

(7) Literature as the flower of language; reflections of a national ideal; unique contributions of French, German, Russian, and Spanish authors to world literature.

(8) A survey of music, opera, art, architecture, and films of major language cultures.

(9) Language and beyond; computer languages and natural languages; possibilities of artificial intelligence; language as thought-conditioner in advertising, philosophy, and rhetoric; the language of symbols and signs (semiotics); codes.
[Keller and Ferguson, 1976, p. 51.]

The organizers have assembled their own text which incorporates the materials from various sources used in course handouts. They consider the diversity of material covered and the necessarily brief treatment of some topics to be *minor* problems.

The University of Maryland
(Baltimore County Campus) Model

Language faculty members at the Catonsville Campus of the University of Maryland have designed a core of courses which encompasses general linguistics, the phenomenon of language, and types of language, that is, styles and usage (*On Campus*, May 1979). (See the *Modern Language Journal*, Autumn 1984, pp. 222-29.)

"The World of Language" is a pair of single-semester courses which may be taken independently or together. It is part of a core of three courses aimed at both language majors and the student population at large. Language majors are strongly urged to take one semester of "The World of Language."

The other two parts of the triad of courses are "World Language Communities" and "Textual Analysis." The emphasis in the former is on the introduction to the study of language in a broad context of historical, political, and social issues. It examines various theories of the origin of language and the nature of language from the points of view of Whorf, Sapir, Chomsky, and Skinner. The geography of language, language families, and the issue of language minorities are also considered in this course.

In the third course, "Textual Analysis," students are introduced to semiotics, the study of signs and symbols. They examine a wide variety of texts for the purpose of interpretation and analysis of written messages in relation to visual codes.

Communication theory—messages, codes, sending and receiving—is the organizing factor in this course. Nonmajors work with English; foreign language majors work with French, German, and Spanish texts (*Forum*, October 1980, p. 7).

The types of courses described in these two models can contribute much to the content preparation of language teachers, for both exploratory and sequential language programs.

Preservice and in-service teachers who are interested in exploratory-type programs should inquire of the foreign language department or college of education at their institutions. (Additional samples are listed in the Appendix of this text.)

An Exploratory Methods Course

The resurgence of exploratory language instruction in the secondary school curriculum requires not only that prospective language teachers be knowledgeable in the pertinent content but also that they be proficient in teaching that content. The following description of a methods course which was designed specifically for prospective and current secondary school teachers of foreign language exploratory courses is easily adaptable to the methods and content of a similar course for the post-secondary level.

In the Spring of 1979, the University of Maryland, College Park, offered a course on the "Organization and Implementation of the Exploratory Foreign Language Course in the Secondary School." The course included both theory and practice. Theory was presented through lectures, outside readings, and the original, unpublished version of this text. By designing the course so that it simulated an actual exploratory course, students experienced the practical application of the underlying theory. In addition to readings on the history, rationale, scope, design, and implementation of exploratory courses, participants were required to develop and collect actual content material and information. The material, both linguistic and cultural in nature, was gleaned from texts, magazines, newspapers, native informants, content and area colleagues, secondary school exploratory teachers, and cultural field trips. After the content was gathered, students, either individually of in teams, presented a lesson to the class. These lessons included cultural "tidbits"; sample language information in Hausa, German, Hebrew, Chinese, and other languages; Morse code; sign language; instructional games; simulated cultural clashes; and a host of other similar activities. Several student and guest speaker presentations were videotaped for future use.

As a culminating activity, all participants contributed to a multicultural social. The course instructor took advantage of the multiethnic composition of the class: participants brought main dishes, desserts, snacks, beverages, and music which were native to their cultural origins. A by-product of this activity was the beginning of a cross-cultural cookbook which was available to students in other courses throughout the area.

The foregoing description exemplifies possible activities which the authors recommend as part of the exploratory language course. By completing the exploratory methods course, future and current foreign language teachers experienced, in essence, the actual exploratory curriculum.

In-Service Education for Exploratory Teachers

Since many middle or junior high school exploratory course teachers have not had the benefit of a formal exploratory methods course, program coordinators or school administrators must establish a plan for the course instructors' orientation and training.

Teachers continue to acquire both the skills and content while they are involved in teaching exploratory courses. However, it is important that exploratory teachers understand the concept and related procedures *before* they begin. In order for teachers to feel that they are responsible for implementing *with* students a course with a specific body of knowledge, skills, and attitudes, the school system must first define and document, through its curriculum processes, the nature of the particular type of exploratory course which it intends to implement. The rationale, goals, and objectives, with the organizational framework of the course, should be clearly stated. Furthermore, teachers must understand the administrative organization and policies related to a course of this type.

A Package of Strategies

The orientation and training of the in-service exploratory teacher can be effected through a number of strategies within the available time frame. This task has been accomplished through:

- Workshops
- Individual orientation
- Observation of an effective teacher as a model
- Viewing videotaped class sessions (less desirable than observation of a live model)
- Requirement of a teacher plan for the course. (See samples which follow.)

Workshops can include:

- Presentations in content and methods by experienced teachers, community resource persons, and supervisors/coordinators/specialists.
- Discussions
- Simulations
- Examination of representative teaching materials
- Handouts (The main items of background material might be mailed to participants for their study *before* the workshop.)
- Preparation of some materials according to individual needs
- Assistance in formulating a long-range teaching plan
- Help in pronouncing less familiar language(s) which may arise in the exploratory class.

Samples

Chapter 4 contained broad guidelines for methodology and teacher training. Samples of materials which were actually employed in the orientation and training of exploratory teachers in the schools of Prince George's County, Maryland, are presented on the following pages. The authors present the following items which are included in the aforenoted materials. The reader is free to utilize these items *in toto* or to excerpt them. (For bibliographic information on resources listed in the samples, see chapter 6.)

1. Plan for a pre-school workshop
2. Course conceptualization for teachers
3. A helpful approach to course planning
4. Daily lesson plans
5. Project suggestions
6. Sample teacher's long-range plan.

Sample 1: Pre-School Workshop for Exploratory One day (can be expanded to two days)

Agenda Summary

A.M.

- Overall course
- Content
- Linguistic categories in curriculum guide
- Guidelines for organizing content material
- Basic lesson format
- Sample lesson plan/questions

P.M.

- Exploratory timetable (semester/year)
- Materials discussion and examination
- Homework/study skills/grading
- Grouping of students in class
- Academic standards
- Discipline/behavior
- Help with German (for French and Spanish majors)
- Help with Latin (for teachers not familiar)
- Participants in work groups
    (Preparing individual course plan for a year or semester)
- Recapitulation/feedback

All agenda activities are led by supervisors, successful teachers, and special resource persons.

Agenda Elaboration

9:00-10:00

Discussion of: Course concepts to be developed with students; vehicle for content, e.g., "Making Friends," "Dining," "Travel," etc., French, Spanish culture

REFERENCES TO PAGES IN CURRICULUM GUIDE THROUGHOUT

10:00-11:30: GUIDELINES FOR ORGANIZING

Outline of recommended class period

First Segment:	(1) Teaching selected foreign expressions
	(2) Connections to English
	(3) Sources for content
Second Segment:	(1) General language material (language history, roots, etc.)
	(2) Methods for working with culture (Avoidance of lecture approach) • Group work for individual/class projects • Library skills • Reporting skills (Projects involve language, culture, and career education)
	(3) Specific activities for class and homework
	(4) Career education component
	(5) Testing
Third Segment:	(1) Planning *with* students—assign homework
	(2) Evaluate *with* students (Reference to pages in *Guide*)
	(3) Quick review of phrases taught in the First Segment, with questions about English connections
	(4) Learning of songs

11:30-12:00:	Sample Lesson Plan/Questions
1:00-1:30:	Exploratory calendar, materials, study skills, grading, methodology, grouping, discipline Standards for oral and written reports
1:30-2:30:	Help with Latin and German pronunciation
2:30-3:45:	*Participants in work groups* *Tasks:* Planning the first week or Beginning work on year's plan
3:45-4:00:	Recapitulation

Sample 2: Course Conceptualization for Teachers

EXPLORATORY FOREIGN LANGUAGE—MORE THAN "MAINSTREAM CHIC"

Rationale and Goals
for
Exploratory Course which Combines General Language and Foreign Language Sampling

READINESS for Classroom Foreign Language Study

Most elementary school children have no foreign language experiences; consequently, many pupils of middle school age are not prepared to cope with the exigencies of Level I; the exploratory experience develops readiness for language study.

LINGUISTIC/CULTURAL AWARENESS

The exploratory course may represent the only exposure to other languages and cultures for those pupils who will never study a foreign language sequentially.

Exploratory Course Conceptualization (Teacher Handout). Prince George's County Schools, Upper Marlboro, Maryland. Reprinted by permission.

NATIVE LANGUAGE SKILLS CONNECTIONS

The course contributes to the pupils' general education and provides another dimension in English skill development.

PERSONAL DEVELOPMENT/DECISION MAKING
CAREER AWARENESS—HANDS-ON

Having been exposed to several languages, the pupil is better equipped to make a reasoned decision concerning formal language study. The course is in harmony with the exploratory philosophy of the middle school level and awareness phase of career education.

_____GOALS_____

COGNITIVE/PSYCHOMOTOR

- nature and history of language
- limited skills in specific languages
- foreign elements of English
- specific cultures—including U.S.A.
- language learning *process*
- languages—world of work

AFFECTIVE

Positive Attitudes:
- other cultures
- other tongues
- language study
- work
- U.S.A. heritage
- service

EXPLORATORY CONCEPT
FOR TEACHERS

CONCEPTS: *About* language, *about* culture, *about* career development			
(1)	(2)	(3)	(4)
General Language and Relationship to English Language Skills	1. Foreign Language Samples ---2. Pre-Level I Skills	Cultures	Career Awareness

1. Every day in some manner something from *each box* should be included in the teacher's plan.

2. The *Samples* and *Cultures* boxes are more closely connected in the drawing because the culture studied emanates from the language being sampled.

Sample 3: A Helpful Approach to Course Planning

How to Approach Planning and Teaching FLEX*
in Prince George's County, Maryland

(Teacher Handout)

Points

I.   It is important to understand that FLEX is a course about Spanish and French cultures and the relationship of these cultures and their languages to English.

II. This course has many books; however, there are three major books students will use. They are:
1) *General Language*[3]
2) *Berlitz Spanish/French for Travelers*
3) *France* or *Mexico* (Scott, Foresman and Company)

III. As resources for planning, teachers may use many materials; however, essential tools are:
1) The *Exploratory Resource Guide*
2) Foreign Language—*Middle School Guide*
3) *Instructional Activity Packets:*
     a. Mexican Scene
     b. Teacher-made resource units
     c. Lingua Latina Mortua Non Est (*Latin Is Not Dead*)[4]
     d. Word List Diagrams
     e. Dictionary Activities
     f. Foreign Language Borrowings Used in Media—"Media Literacy"
     g. Materials explaining codes, such as Morse code, musical symbols, computer languages

---

*Acronym sometimes used for *Foreign Language Exploratory*.

[3]The text *General Language* is published by Holt, Rinehart & Winston. Although it is currently out of print, school systems may write to the publisher for permission to reprint.

[4]This packet is listed in chapter 6.

Teacher handout reprinted by permission of originator—Patricia Barr-Harrison.

IV. All lessons are planned through four major linguistic categories (for each language explored)

September   1) Making Friends
Oct.-Nov.   2) Travel, Cars and Driving, Numbers and Time, Shopping and Services
Nov.-Dec.   3) Dining and Food Concepts in Cultures
                4) Holidays, Festivals, Sports
                (Repeat categories for new language second semester)

The teacher should decide, based on the *Resource Guide*, what aspects of the culture should be learned by students within the timetable. There should be performance objectives written in two-week segments. The *foreign phrases* will then relate to the culture or through situational dialogues or circumstances. The daily lesson plan will be based on the two-week plan, which will help teachers reach all of their objectives by the end of the study of linguistic categories.

Each day, the lesson plan will contain:
1) Foreign Language—Linguistics
2) General Language
3) Foreign Culture
   (Career Education activities as appropriate)

Sample 4-a: Daily Lesson Plans

Foreign Language Exploratory

(Teacher Handout)

Sample Lesson Plan

I. **Language**   **Materials Needed**

Introduce Spanish   Buenos días
  greetings: Buenas tardes
• oral repetition   Buenas noches   • Dittoed
• visual presentation   Adiós   expressions
• no writing   Hasta mañana
                        Hasta tarde   • Slide presentation
                        ¿Cómo está Ud.?   with short
                        Estoy bien, gracias.   dialogue
                        ¿Cómo te llamas?

Teacher handout reprinted by permission of originator—Roberta Dondes Stein.

II. **English Connection** (Latin)
    die(s)—day—per diem
    bonus—good—bonus
    nox, noctis—night—nocturnal
    bene—well—beneficial, benefaction, benefactor, benefit,
      beneficiary

III. **Culture**
    (1) "How Spaniards and Latin   • Reading selection
        Americans greet one another."
        Reading and comprehension
        questions. Brief discussion of how
        Spaniards and Latin Americans
        greet one another and in what
        ways those cultures are similar to
        and different from the habits of
        Americans (U.S.). How would it
        make you feel to greet a person in
        that fashion? Why would you feel
        that way? Practice on your
        neighbor.

    (2) Spain—geographical overview   • Individual desk maps
        group work—locate and label
        various places in Spain: major   • Large classroom map
        cities and waterways

                                         • Overhead transparency

IV. **Summary and Review**
    Spanish Expressions   - matching quiz on overhead transparency
                              - BINGO
                              - Class repetition of expressions
    Spanish Alphabet

    Homework: *General Language*—read pp. 177-79, "Reasons for
                Studying Spanish." On paper, list the reasons the
                author enumerates for studying Spanish. Can you
                think of any others?

Alternate Activities
    Use Berlitz books to look up Spanish greetings
    Movie/film on Spanish cultures
    Word derivation/borrowing activity
    Speaker from Spain (life in Spain, customs, etc.)

Sample 4-b: Daily Lesson Plans

Foreign Language Exploratory

(Teacher Handout)

Sample Lesson Plan

I. **Language**

Review greetings: Bonjour, etc.
Introduce: Quel temps fait-il?
                   il fait froid   (Use flashcards or
                   il fait beau   pictures to illustrate.)
                   il fait chaud

II. **English Connection**
temps—temperate, temperature
froid—freezing, refrigerator, frigid
beau—beautiful, beautify

III. **Review France Geographically—on Overhead**
Students follow with their maps
What is the shape of France?
Name the capital, etc. . .

IV. **Discussion**
What is France's cultural importance?
When you think of France, what crosses your mind?
Discuss France's luxury items: e.g., perfumes, jeans, wines
Career planning—how might French be helpful to anyone working
     in a department store?

V. **General Language Book**—Chapter 11, page 205.
Read questions 1 and 2 for discussion.

VI. **Summary and Review**
Quickly go over phrases practiced in Part I.
Homework: Look up and write a dictionary definition of
     temperature.
Read over map for possible quiz.

Teacher handout reprinted by permission of originator—Nadia Wasserman.

In Parts III and IV: Substitute activity could be:

- having the class listen to a few reports based on projects
- engaging in project work in the library or classroom (small groups) and individual work with *previously set* standards of operation.

Sample 5-a: Project Suggestions

Foreign Language Exploratory

(Teacher Handout)

General Student Guidelines for Preparing Projects

I. **Decide What Your Goals Are**

What is the purpose of this project?

II. **Give Specific Instructions**

- length of report
- pen or pencil
- neatness
- originality of presentation (no copying directly from the encyclopedia; illustrations)
- teach *how* to *use* the encyclopedia
- suggest approach (skits, report, journal, etc.)
- bibliography
- show samples, if possible
- oral report (no reading word for word, may use notes; explain new words to audience before beginning report)
- due dates:
  two dates: 1. for approach and topic approval
  2. final due date

Do not assume pupils possess research skills.

III. **Make Materials Available**

1. library time
2. classroom time
3. use of other students/teachers/community members

Teacher handout reprinted by permission of originator—Nadia Wasserman.

IV. **Criteria for Grading**

> Example: 50% content
> 25% oral presentation
> 25% neatness, originality

Sample 5-b: Project Suggestions

Foreign Language Exploratory

(Teacher Handout)

Sample Project Topic

French-Speaking Countries—Travel Brochure

I. **Goals:**   -To familiarize students with the number of French-speaking countries
-To acquaint students with materials available in the library
-To help students organize ideas and present them orally.

II. **Below is a list of French-speaking countries outside of France**

Canada (Quebec Province)	Monaco	Niger	Guinea
	Tunisia	Mauritania	French Guyana
	Corsica	Mali	Dahomey
Haiti	Morocco	Senegal	Togo
Guadeloupe	Algeria	Upper Volta	Cameroon
Martinique	Chad	Ivory Coast	Gabon
Belgium	Laos	Republic of the Congo	
Luxemburg	Vietnam	Madagascar	
Switzerland	Cambodia	Zaire	
	Lebanon		

III. Choose one country and write your own *travel brochure*. Be sure to include information on the following:

geography	climate	clothing
history	language	transportation
sports	cuisine (food)	interesting sights

You must include a *bibliography*.

Teacher handout reprinted by permission of originator—Nadia Wasserman.

IV. You will be graded on the content, neatness, and originality. Use maps, drawings, pictures, etc. You will be taken to the library twice and class time will be available. You must also present a *short* oral summary of your report. You may not *read* it, but you may use notes.

Sample 5-c: Project Suggestions

Foreign Language Exploratory

(Teacher Handout)

Career Lab Project

I. **Goals:**   -To acquaint students with materials available in the career lab
-To analyze their career choice
-To see the usefulness of a foreign language in their career choice.

II. **Directions:**

Using the *Occupational Outlook Handbook* and any other material available to you, answer the following questions. Be sure to use a pen and to answer in complete sentences. *Neatness* is important. You are required to prepare a *bibliography*.

1. What is your chosen career?

2. What are its educational requirements?

3. What is its employment outlook? Where would you most likely be able to find employment? (What areas of the country?)

4. What are its salary and chances of advancement?

5. How might the knowledge of a foreign language be useful?

6. Write an ad for your chosen occupation. Be sure to refer to your notes and to the ad section of the newspaper. Newspapers will be available in class.

Teacher handout reprinted by permission of originator—Nadia Wasserman.

Teacher Long-Range Plan. Exploratory program coordinators can assist new teachers in understanding the exploratory concept and organizing their classroom instruction by requiring them to prepare a complete plan for the semester or year. This plan should be submitted to the coordinator prior to the beginning of the school year.

In programs where this procedure was followed, teachers have reported that they were better able to comprehend the course framework and its components.

The following is an actual teacher-prepared year's plan. With the originator's approval, such plans may be distributed at workshops as samples. Not all plans used as models need be so detailed. Some may include a more specific timetable.

Sample 6: Teacher's Long-Range Plan

Basic Outline for Language Exploratory Course

(Teacher Handout)

French and Spanish

I.   **Communicating for World Understanding**   (1st Semester)
      Language Development
        1. Origin of Language
        2. Purpose of Language
        3. Why study a foreign language? (Filmstrip)
           a. Careers
           b. World understanding
           c. Vocabulary development and language skills

II.   **Signs and Symbols**
      A. Origins and Heraldry
        1. Family crest—Make your own.
        2. Sign language—Story of Helen Keller; learn sign language—Sign: Your name, Hello, Goodbye.
        3. Make up a sign language (project).

Teacher handout reprinted by permission of originator—Lynda Folk.

B. **Signs and Symbols in Everyday Life**

1. Business signs
2. Direction signs
3. Advertising signs
4. Career symbols

- Make up a sign advertising a business or career.
- Check phone books, newspapers, magazines, etc. for advertising signs.
- Copy or make up signs used to give directions.

III.   **Families of Languages**
   A. A Language Tree
   B. The family tree (project)
   C. Learn the French alphabet. Spell nouns and names. Spelling bee.
   D. Slanguage,* CB language, terms and expressions pertinent to specific hobbies, e.g., CARS-Model-T, rod, valve ping, etc.

IV.   **French Language** (Will have been started with Part I.) (ongoing)
   A. **Making Friends**
      1. Greetings
      2. Introductions and identification

   B. **Numbers, Time, and the Weather**
      1. Clock—Telling time on the hour, noon, and midnight
      2. International time table
      3. Days, months, seasons—Calendar project
         Days introduced by date: C'est lundi, le 17 décembre
      4. Weather terms—Flashcards or illustrated weather chart.

   C. **Travel**
      1. Transportation—Concentration game/means of transportation
      2. Signs and map reading—International road signs
      3. Passport and customs information—Fill in a passport form; discover pertinent customs information for various French-speaking countries.
      4. Metric system—Plan a trip using kilometers
      5. Places
         a. Places of interest to visit
         b. Stations, hotels, restaurants, etc.
         c. Types of stores, etc.

---

*See *Slanguage, America's Second Language* by Carothers and Lacey, New York: Sterling Pub. Company, 1979.

D. Dining

1. Restaurant etiquette
2. Common names of foods
   - Make a French-English menu
   - Make crepes
   - Make a food picture dictionary
   - Comparison of French/American eating customs and attitudes
   - Make a grocery list.

E. Sports

1. Soccer
2. Bicycle Tour de France—Chart a *Tour de France* on a map of France.
3. Skiing—Alps
4. Follow the athletes from the various French-speaking countries.

F. Shopping

1. Money—Comparison of money in Canada, France, and one of the African countries.
2. Shopping and shops—Make a chart of a typical French street and identify the various shops.
3. Compare shopping customs of the various countries.
4. Clothing, colors, and sizes
   - Compare metric and American sizes
   - Make a color chart
   - Make a clothes chart.

G. Services

1. Identify and state a need for services (traveler, student, resident).
2. Identify international signs and symbols and how and where they are used.
3. Discuss making phone calls, exchanging money, going to a service station, getting medical aid, etc. Prepare a list of common questions asked and information necessary to answer them.

H. Cars and Driving

1. Review road signs.
2. Make a map of a short tour; discuss directions, cost of gas, and measurement of distance and quantities.

3. Review weather information.
4. Make a chart of road signs and information signs helpful for your trip.

I. **Holidays and Festivals**
1. History
2. Folklore, music, dancing—Learn French songs/dances, e.g., "Sur le Pont d'Avignon."
3. Popular customs—Père Noël, les sabots, le 14 Juillet.
4. Christmas, Easter, Tour de France.

J. **Language/Culture Comparison with English**
1. Foreign words commonly used
2. U.S.-French relationships—Louisiana Purchase, exploration, Lafayette, Revolutionary War, Statue of Liberty.
3. Exploration—cities and towns in the U.S. with French names.
4. Language usage, paralanguage, kinesics.

K. **Foreign Visitors and Immigrants**
1. Aids to better understanding—How would you introduce a new student from a foreign country to your school?
2. Welcome—Agencies, tour offices, school, church, etc. Bilingual services—location, duties.

L. **Career Development**
1. Ongoing throughout the semester—Relate to topics and areas being studied, e.g., TRAVEL—travel agent, flight attendant, customs officer, mapmaker, tour guide, etc.
2. Project—Individual investigation of a career and how learning a foreign language might be helpful to the career.
3. Guest speakers—Travel agent, foreign service officer, diplomat, librarian, company official.
4. Flashcards—French/English—careers and occupations.

V. **Rome and the Latin Language**
A. Contributions of Roman civilization
B. Influence of Latin on English and the Romance languages
1. Roots
2. Prefixes
3. Suffixes

  C. Roman numerals
  D. Mythology
  E. Word derivation games
  F. Dictionary search and word origin search

VI. **Greece and the Greek Language**
  A. Contributions of the Greek civilization
  B. Influence on English and the Romance Languages
   1. Roots
   2. Prefixes
   3. Suffixes
  C. Greece and democracy
  D. Greek alphabet (sororities, fraternities; symbols used in math)
  E. Contribution to professional fields—law, philosophy, math, etc.
  F. What's-in-a-Word game.

VII. **Spain and the Spanish Language* (2nd Semester)**
  A. **Spain throughout the World**
   1. Identify on world maps.
   2. Choose your country for individual study.

  B. **Group project—Spain, Mexico, Puerto Rico—**Individual projects on other Spanish-speaking countries.
   1. Comparison culture chart to be kept by each student
   2. Information to be drawn from individual reports, e.g., principal cities, main crop, government, a famous monument.

  C. **Topics of interest for group and individual study**
   1. Geography
   2. Historical background
   3. Major cities
   4. Important monuments
   5. Education and religion
   6. Sports and leisure
   7. Industry
   8. Agriculture
   9. Social structure.

---

*The general language component—items I-III of this outline—is taught at the beginning of the course. It is not repeated the second semester.

D. **Making Friends**
   1. Introductions and greetings—Compare English/French/ Spanish
   2. Identification (nationality, etc.)

E. **Numbers, Time, Weather, and Seasons**
   1. Review international time table
   2. Project—Weather/calendar
      (illustrated daily reports for a month)
   3. Concentration game
   4. Word search game

F. **Family, Home, School, Community, and City**
   1. Family—Illustrate (dolls, pictures, drawings) and identify.
   2. Home—diorama, blueprint sketch—Label, compare Spanish living with American living.
   3. Dictionary of school and classroom items—Illustrate with drawings and pictures.
   4. Name important buildings in a city (town hall, hospital).
   5. Find pictures and label public servants (firefighter, etc.).
   6. Choose a career in Public Service and tell about it.
   7. Construct and label a small town.
   8. Prepare a skit on going to the hospital (or some similar topic).

G. **Clothing, Colors, Sizes, and Money**
   1. Make a color chart.
   2. Compare American and European sizes.
   3. Write a skit about going shopping.
   4. Compare Spanish and American money.

H. **Dining**
   1. Write and present a skit about ordering from a menu.
   2. Make a scrapbook of foods found in a restaurant.
   3. Food shopping
      a. Discuss metric measurements.
      b. Make a shopping list for a picnic or party.
   4. Services and Money
      a. Discuss exchanging American/Spanish money at a bank.
      b. Mail a letter to a friend in Spain, Mexico, or Puerto Rico (name, address, etc., mailing services, stamps).
      c. Telephone etiquette—Write a skit on making a phone call.

I. **Travel**
   1. Passport and customs.
   2. Making reservations (hotel, restaurant, travel).
   3. Transportation: car, taxi, bus, metro.
   4. Make a Concentration game of transportation.
   5. Make a travel game using means of transportation and international road signs.
   6. Plan a trip to a Spanish-speaking country.
      a. Obtain travel information (tourist agency).
      b. Fill in a passport.
      c. Make a route identifying places of interest.

J. **Sports**
   1. Bullfighting
   2. Soccer
   3. Pros and cons of bullfighting (debate)
   4. Follow Spanish and Latin American athletes.

K. **Holidays and Festivals**
   1. Christmas
   2. Easter
   3. Independence days
   4. Fiestas
      a. Make a piñata.
      b. Learn a Spanish fiesta song and dance.
      c. Make holiday food.

L. **Language/Culture Comparison to English**
   1. Spanish words commonly used—Make a list.
   2. Friendship and ties to the U.S.: exploration, energy crisis.
   3. Minority factor in America.

M. **Career Development**
   1. Ongoing throughout the semester
   2. Project—Individual investigation of a career.
   3. Guest speakers—Careers using Spanish

VIII. **Germany and the German Language**
   A. The Germanic Branch of the Indo-European Tree
   B. Germany Yesterday and Today
   C. Borrowings from the German Language

D. Contributions and Achievements
E. Common Greetings
F. Numbers, Seasons, Days, and Months
G. Why is the study of the German language of importance to a student of English?
H. Plan a tour of Germany. Talk about the importance of the Rhine. List a few of the highlights of the country.
I. Learn a Bavarian dance and song.
J. Name other German-speaking areas.

Chapter 6

Representative Materials and Resources

Exploratory teachers are persistently confronted by the lack of readily available materials and resources for the course. Before implementing an exploratory course, administrators and staff should secure sufficient materials to be utilized for content instruction. In addition, there should be an organized set of *student* materials for each class member. These materials might consist of a basic text,[1] texts on various countries, and appropriate preplanned copies or duplicated print and nonprint materials.

The authors, who collectively have many years of elementary and secondary school teaching experience, note that administrators, parents, and students tend to view "textless" courses with less esteem than those in which an approved set of student texts and/or other student materials are employed. Additionally, by providing the students with a core set of materials, the teacher can enhance the secure atmosphere which students seek when they enter a new field of study. The authors base their view on the assumption that all students benefit from having a uniform set of materials, which signals at least minimal criteria for completing a particular course. Of course, resources should be adaptable to individual needs.

In an attempt to respond to this issue, the authors have assembled a listing of suggested materials and resources which should be made available to teachers and students. The authors advise course instructors that one of the teaching strategies in the exploratory course is to have students create some of their own materials. If acceptable, these in turn can become part of the classroom pool of resources.

---

[1] For example, *General Language (English and Its Foreign Relations)*, Holt, Rinehart, & Winston. Although this book is out of print, permission to duplicate the entire text may be obtained by writing to the publisher at 383 Madison Avenue, New York, NY 10017.

Principal Materials

The specific materials listed in this chapter comprised the core of the exploratory program in the schools of Prince George's County, Maryland. They were supplied to each of the participating schools. In addition to providing basic content for the pupils, some of the materials were useful as sources of information for those teachers whose knowledge about language was limited to their own teaching specialty. They are presented here as an *example* of a basic set of materials for the exploratory curriculum.

For General Language Development

1. **Text:** *General Language: English and Its Foreign Relations*

   Lilly Lindquist and Clarence Wachner
   (with teacher's manual) *One copy per pupil.*
   Holt, Rinehart & Winston
   383 Madison Avenue
   New York, New York 10017

2. **Filmstrips/Cassettes:** *Linguistic Backgrounds of English*

   Society for Visual Education
   1345 Diversey Parkway
   Chicago, Illinois 60614
   (Though now out of print, this set is in many school libraries.)

3. **Filmstrip/Discs:** *Speaking of Language*

   Guidance Associates
   Communications Park
   Box 300
   White Plains, N.Y. 10602
   (Consult catalog for other language materials)

4. **Posters/Charts:** "Derivative Tree"
   (Latin and Greek elements in English words; Latin abbreviations; and the Greek alphabet)

   American Classical League Service Bureau
   Miami University
   Oxford, Ohio 45056

5. **Packet for Teachers:** *Lingua Latina Mortua Non Est*
   (Latin Is Not Dead) by Lauren Pearl and Dora Kennedy

American Classical League Service Bureau
Miami University
Oxford, Ohio 45056

6. **Wall Map:** *Languages of the World*
Rand McNally
P.O. Box 7600
Chicago, Illinois 60680

7. **Metric:** *Metric System Charts* (Role of Latin and Greek prefixes in the metric system vocabulary)

David C. Cook Company
School Products Division
Elgin, Illinois 60120

For Specific Languages and Cultures

(French, Hispanic, and German)

1. **Texts:**
   a. *French for Travelers*
      German for Travelers
      Spanish for Travelers (2 versions: Latin American and Peninsular)

   Berlitz Publications, Inc.
   866 Third Avenue
   New York, New York 10022

   b. *People of the World Series*
          France - *one per student*
          Mexico - *one per student*

   Scott, Foresman and Company
   99 Bauer Drive
   Oakland, New Jersey 07436

   (Several other countries available)

   c. McDonald Countries - *classroom sets*
          France
          Spain
          West Germany
          Canada
          Mexico

Silver Burdett Company
250 James Street
Morristown, New Jersey 07960

d. *Time-Life Books on Countries*

Silver Burdett Company
250 James Street
Morristown, New Jersey 07960

(Though now out of print, these books are in many school and public libraries.)

e. *Foods and Cooking - one of each*
Time-Life Series
Spain/Portugal
Latin America
Caribbean Isles
France
Africa
Germany
Switzerland
Austria

Silver Burdett Company
250 James Street
Morristown, New Jersey 07960

f. *Travel and Culture Guides*—latest editions—*one of each* (Fodor)
France, Spain, Caribbean, Mexico, South America, Canada

David McKay Company
750 Third Avenue
New York, New York 10018

(Travel Guides are also available from Berlitz Publications, Inc.)

g. *Culture Capsules*
World Culture Series:
USA - Mexico
USA - France
USA - Germany

Newbury House
Rowley, Massachusetts 01969

h. *Culturgrams*
Brigham Young University
Center for International
and Area Studies
Provo, Utah 84602

i. *French Teenager*
German Teenager
Spanish Teenager

American Language Teacher
Box 07300
Detroit, Michigan 48207

j. *Readings in the History and Culture of Puerto Rico*

Continental Press
Elizabethtown, Pennsylvania 17022

k. *Viva! Mexican Americans*

Steck-Vaughn Company
P.O. Box 2028
Austin, Texas 78768
(Classroom set)

l. *These Strange German Ways*

German Information Center
410 Park Avenue
New York, New York 10022
(Classroom sets)

2. **Cultural Posters:** *Living in Puerto Rico* (with teacher manual)

Silver Burdett Company
(See Item c above for address)

3. **Filmstrips/Tapes/Discs/Cassettes:**
a. *Why Study Foreign Languages?*

New York State Association of
Foreign Language Teachers
1102 Ardsley Rd.
Schenectady, N.Y. 12308

b. *Why Study French?*
American Association of Teachers of
French (AATF)

Gessler Publishing Company
900 Broadway
New York, N.Y. 10003

c. *People of the Caribbean*

Learning Arts
P.O. Box 179
Wichita, Kansas 76201

d. *Puerto Rico and the Puerto Ricans*

Learning Arts
(See above.)

e. *Un Viaje por Mexico* (A Trip through Mexico)

Holt, Rinehart and Winston (1970)
383 Madison Avenue
New York, New York 10017

f. *Voici la France* (Here Is France)

Holt, Rinehart and Winston (1970)
(See above.)

(Although it is no longer published, it may be found in some school libraries or foreign language departments. Items g and h are suggested as substitutes.)

g. *Understanding Mexico*

Educational Filmstrips
Huntsville, Texas 77340

h. *Passport to France*
Passport to Mexico
Passport to Spain
Passport to Germany

EMC Publishing
180 East Sixth Street
Saint Paul, Minnesota 55101

i. *Spain*

Educational Filmstrips
(See Item g above for address.)

j. *Berlitz-Pathescope Travel Series*
    French
    Spanish   Set #1
    German

    Pathescope Industrial Media
    71 Weyman Avenue
    New Rochelle, New York 10802

    (Though not of recent vintage, these filmstrips present useful travel and shopping vocabulary.)

4. **Wall/Desk Maps:** France, Latin America, Spain, Quebec, Africa, World, W. Germany, Caribbean

    Rand McNally
    P.O. Box 7600
    Chicago, Illinois 60680

5. **Student Newspapers: Bonjour, Qué tal, Das Rad**

    Scholastic Foreign Language Services
    904 Sylvan Avenue
    Englewood, New Jersey 07632

    (For exposure, not fluent reading.)

6. **Music:** *Spanish American Music and its Roots*

    Text and disc

    Silver Burdett Company
    250 James Street
    Morristown, New Jersey 07960

For Career Development

Awareness and Exploration:

1. *Foreign Languages and Your Career*
    Edward Bourgoin, 1984

    Columbia Language Services
    P.O. Box 28365
    Washington, D.C. 20005

2. *Career Education in the Academic Classroom*
Mangum and Baker (Editors), 1975

   Olympus Publishing Company
Salt Lake City, Utah

3. *Career Education: What It Is and How To Do It*
Hoyt and Evans

   Olympus Publishing Company
(See above for address.)

4. *Foreign Language Box*

   Houghton Mifflin Publishing Company
Pennington-Hopewell Rd.
Hopewell, New Jersey 08525

5. *Exploring Careers in Foreign Language*
(Spirit Masters)

   J. Weston Walch
Box 658
Portland, Maine 04104

6. *Foreign Languages in Careers* (One per school)
New York State Association of Foreign Language
Teachers (1977)
1102 Ardsley Road
Schenectady, New York, 12308

7. *ACTFL Career Sampler*

8. *Foreign Languages and Your Career* (tape/slide presentation)

9. *Perfect Infusion—Foreign Languages* (Film)
All the above from:

   ACTFL
358 Warburton Ave.
Hastings-on-Hudson, New York 10706

Additional Teacher Sources

1. *National Geographic*—School Library Collection
17th and M St., N.W.
Washington, D.C. 20036

   (Other magazines and newspapers as appropriate.)

2. *School System Curriculum Guides:*
   Prince George's County Schools
   Instructional Service Bldg.
   Upper Marlboro, Maryland 20772
   a. *Foreign Language Exploratory*
      Resource Guide & Handbook
   b. *Foreign Language—Middle School*
   c. *Career Education and Foreign Languages*
   d. *Latin Curriculum Guide*
   e. *Latin and the World of Work*

3. *The Miracle of Language*
   Charlton Laird, 1953

   Fawcett Publications
   Greenwich, Connecticut

In addition to the materials provided systemwide, teachers had access to the resources of their own schools and communities for realia, class speakers, and field trips (to restaurants, museums, embassies, business establishments, etc.).

Addendum to List of Principal Materials

The following is a general listing of materials that are not included in either the foregoing list or the bibliography for this book. For the convenience of the reader, the listing is divided into cultural and pedagogical topics.

French Culture

Comeau, R.F.; F.L. Bustin; and N.J. Lamoureux. *Ensemble: Culture et Société.* New York: Holt, Rinehart and Winston, 1977.

D'Amecourt and N. Germain. *Savoir-vivre.* Ottawa: Les Editions de l'Homme, Ltée., 1969.

Gregoir, H., And J. Talandier. *Vins Français.* Paris: Grange Batelière, 1972.

Hilton, L.M. *France: Comparative Culture and Government.* Lincolnwood, IL: National Textbook Co., 1971.

Hilton, L.M. *France: Its People and Culture,* Focus on Europe Series. Lincolnwood, IL: National Textbook Co., 1981.

Ladu, T.T. *What Makes the French French.* Detroit: Advancement Press of America, 1974.

Piem, and F. Tomich. *The French and the Nation.* Paris: La Documentation Française, 1980.

Westervelt, W.O. *Belgium: Its People and Culture,* Focus on Europe Series. Lincolnwood, IL: National Textbook Co., 1979.

Methods in Teaching French Culture

Jorstad, H.L. and H.N. Seelye. *The Magazine: French Mini-Culture Unit.* Lincolnwood, IL: National Textbook Co., 1976.

Levno, A.W. *Rencontres Culturelles: Cross-Cultural Mini-Dramas.* Lincolnwood, IL: National Textbook Co., 1977, 1981.

Meeting Another Culture through Language: French. Towson, MD: Board of Education of Baltimore County, 1972.

Culture of Francophone Countries

Douyon, E. *Culture et Développement en Haïti.* Quebec: Editions Lemeac Inc., 1972.

Institut Pédagogique Africain et Malgache. *Géographie: Cours Moyen.* Strasbourg: ISTRA, 1970.

O'Farrell, M. *Quebec at a Glance.* Government of Quebec: Department of Intergovernmental Affairs, 1980.

Peron, Y., and V. Zalacain. *Atlas de la Haute-Volta.* Paris: Editions Jeune Afrique, 1975.

Quebec: A Whole Different World Next Door. Quebec: Tourisme Quebec, 1978.

Rogus, T. *Visages du Québec.* Lincolnwood, IL: National Textbook Co., 1981.

Slater, M.K. *The Caribbean Family: Legitimacy in Martinique.* New York: St. Martin's Press, Inc., 1977.

Weil, T.E. *Area Handbook for Haiti.* Washington, D.C.: U.S. Government Printing Office, 1973.

Culture of Spain

Bawcutt, G.J. *Spanish Sign Language.* London: George G. Harrap & Co. Ltd., 1980.

Daniel, F. *Una mirada a España.* Lincolnwood, IL: National Textbook Co., 1975, 1982.

Gorden, R.L. *Spanish Personal Names.* Yellow Springs, OH: Antioch College, 1968.

Hilton, L.M. *Spain: Its People and Culture,* Focus on Europe Series. Lincolnwood, IL: National Textbook Co., 1980.

Ladu, T.T. *What Makes the Spanish Spanish.* Detroit: Advancement Press of America, Inc., 1974.

Newton, M.T. *Life in a Spanish Town.* London: George G. Harrap & Co. Ltd., 1974, 1980.

Strand, W.E. *Exploring Spain.* New York: Exposition Press, Inc., 1959.

Methods in Teaching Hispanic Culture

Campa, A.L. *Teaching Hispanic Culture through Folklore.* Modern Language Association of America, ERIC Focus Report #2.

Green, J.R. *A Gesture Inventory for the Teaching of Spanish.* Chilton Co., 1968.

Greif, J. and S. Stone. *Mexicans Don't Always Eat Tacos.* Hawthorne, CA: Media for Education, 1979.

Seelye, H.N. *A Handbook on Latin America for Teachers: Methodology and Annotated Bibliography.* Illinois: Office of the Superintendent of Pulbic Instruction, Illinois Title III, NDEA Program, 1968.

Seelye, H.N. *Perspectives for Teachers of Latin American Culture.* Springfield, IL: Division of Instruction, Illinois Title III, NDEA Program, 1970.

Seelye, H.N. and J.L. Day. *The Newspaper: A Reflection of Life-styles in the Spanish-speaking World.* Lincolnwood, IL: National Textbook Co., 1978.

Seelye, H.N. *Teaching Cultural Concepts in Spanish Classes.* Springfield, IL: Office of the Superintendent of Public Instruction, 1972.

Snyder, B. *Encuentros culturales: Cross-Cultural Mini-Dramas.* Lincolnwood, IL: National Textbook Co., 1975, 1980.

The University of the State of New York. *Puerto Rican Resource Units.* Albany, NY: The State Education Dept., Bureau of Migrant Education, 1976.

Culture of Hispanic Countries

Burnett, J. *Muchas facetas de México.* Lincolnwood, IL: National Textbook Co., 1981.

Ferguson, J.H. *The River Plate Republics: Argentina, Paraguay, Uruguay.* New York: Time, Inc., 1968.

Gorden, R.L. *American Guests in Colombian Homes: A Study in Cross-Cultural Communication*. Yellow Springs, OH, and Washington, D.C.: Antioch College and U.S. Office of Education.

Gorden, R.L. *Living in Latin America*. Lincolnwood, IL: National Textbook Co., in conjunction with ACTFL, 1974.

Martinez, G.T. and J. Edwards. *The Mexican American*. Boston: Houghton Mifflin Co., 1973.

Moquin, W. and C. Van Doren. *A Documentary History of the Mexican Americans*. New York: Praeger Publishers, Inc., 1971.

Overholt, K.D. *Voces de Puerto Rico*. Lincolnwood, IL: National Textbook Co., 1981.

Vásquez, R. *Chicano*. New York: Avon Publishers, 1970.

Wagenheim, K. *Puerto Rico: A Profile*. New York: Praeger Publishers, Inc., 1970.

Weil, T.E. *Area Handbook for Colombia*. Washington, D.C.: U.S. Government Printing Office, 1970.

German Culture and Teaching German Culture

Culver, A.I. and H.N. Seelye. *The Magazine: German Mini-Culture Unit*. Lincolnwood, IL: National Textbook Co., 1976.

Facts about Germany. Bonn: Press and Information Office of the Government of the Federal Republic of Germany, 1975.

Sawers, R. *Life in a West German Town*. London: George G. Harrap & Co. Ltd., 1980.

Schwelien, J.H. *Encounter and Encouragement: A Bicentennial Review of German-American Relations*. Bonn: Bonner Universitäts-Buchdruckerei, 1976.

Shirer, R.K. *Kulturelle Begegnungen: Cross-Cultural Mini-Dramas*. Lincolnwood, IL: National Textbook Co., 1981.

Italian Culture and Teaching Italian Culture

Guzzetta-Jones, A. and J. Antinoro-Polizzi. *Diceva la mia nonna (My Grandmother Used to Say)*. Rochester, NY: Heritage Press, 1979.

Kubly, H. *Italy*. New York: Time, Inc., 1961.

Lawson, C.D. *Nuove Letture di Cultura Italiana*. Lincolnwood, IL: National Textbook Co., 1981.

Rallo, J.A. *The Newspaper: Italian Mini-Culture Unit*. Lincolnwood, IL: National Textbook Co., 1976.

Japanese Culture

Japan—Culturgram: Communication Aid. Provo, UT: Brigham Young University, 1982.

Japan (Macdonald Countries). Morristown, NJ: Silver Burdett, 1976.

Japan (Fodor's Guide). New York: David McKay, 1984.

Peck, I. *Japan.* New York: Scholastic Book Services, 1981.

Shiratori, R. *Japan in the Eighties.* New York: Kodansha: Harper & Row, 1983.

Korean Culture

Adams, E. B. *Korea Guide.* Westfield, NJ: Eastview Editors, 1979.

Korea (Fodor's Guide). New York: David McKay, 1983.

Korea in Pictures. New York: Sterling Publishing Company, 1968.

Thai Culture

Nicol, G. *Thailand.* New York: Hippocrene Books, 1980.

Chinese Culture

Garsid, E. *China Companion.* Mystic, CT: Verry Pub. 1981.

Jennings, J. E. (Ed.) *China.* Grand Rapids, MI: Fideler, 1984.

Kimball, R. L. *China Beginner's Traveler's Dictionary.* San Francisco: China Books, Inc., 1980.

The World Book Encyclopedia: China. Chicago: World Book-Childcraft International, Inc., 1980.

Ethnic-American Culture

Reed, R.D. *Series in How and Where to Research Your Ethnic-American Cultural Heritage.* Houston TX: Gulf Publishers, 1981.

Titles in the series: Black Americans; Chinese Americans; German Americans; Irish Americans; Italian Americans; Japanese Americans; Jewish Americans; Mexican Americans; Native Americans; Polish Americans; Russian Americans; Scandinavian Americans.

Vietnamese Culture

Handbook for Teachers of Vietnamese Students. San Antonio, Texas: Intercultural Development Research Association. 1976.

Switzerland

Hilton, L.M. *Switzerland: Its People and Culture,* Focus on Europe Series. Lincolnwood, IL: National Textbook Co., 1981.

This list is a limited one, intended only to *suggest* the wide possibilities of resources. For an increasingly comprehensive and current view, especially on China and Japan, other sources or systems, e.g., ERIC, should be consulted, in public and university libraries.

Chapter 7

Observations and Future Considerations

This book does not represent a final statement in the organization and implementation of exploratory curriculum. The profession should continue to question, investigate, and refine the purpose, content, and design of this type of curriculum. With this in mind, the authors pose the following questions for further study, discussion, and development.

1. Are exploratory "graduates" more successful in Level I than their counterparts of equal ability who have not had the experience?
2. Is there less attrition in beginning levels as a result of the exploratory program?
3. How does the exploratory experience affect pupil performance and attitude in English and social studies?
4. Are pupils of the opinion that the course has really helped them make a more realistic decision about which language to study?
5. Is there more acceptance and less antipathy toward other languages and cultures among exploratory pupils in contrast with other middle school children?
6. How do pupils who have completed an exploratory course compare with those who have completed Level I vis-à-vis questions 3 and 5?
7. Can the exploratory course at the post-secondary level be considered a viable academic course for the general college/ university population and for the education of prospective foreign language teachers?
8. Can a modified exploratory unit be employed during the first two or three weeks of a conventional, Level I foreign language course, in order to orient the beginning student to the *formal* study of language? [This is one suggestion advocated for the infusion of *global education concepts* into the foreign language curriculum (Bragaw et al., 1981, p. 70).]

In addressing these questions, the profession may profit from current trends. Unlike the events which led to the near-demise of the exploratory concept in the late 1940s, present developments may assure its place in foreign language curricula. For example, the exploratory component or course is currently viewed as desirable in a number of applications, most significantly in the global education movement (Bragaw et al., pp. 76, 77) and in the trend toward a multidimensional foreign language curriculum (Stern, 1983, pp. 120-46).

Global education, which has become a mandated program in some states, is explained below, followed by a brief explanation of a proposed multidimensional foreign language curriculum.

The Exploratory Concept in the Emerging Global Awareness Curriculum

Since the publication of the *Report of the President's Commission on Foreign Languages and International Studies*[1], there has been a resurgence of interest in the study of foreign languages and cultures, also reinforced by various commissions studying secondary education. (For example, the President's Commission on Excellence in Education: "A Nation at Risk," 1983.)

The commission report dealing with foreign languages directed the attention of the profession to the global education movement by virtue of its focus on international studies and its specific recommendations for closer collaboration between foreign language teachers and teachers of other subjects, particularly social studies (*Strength through Wisdom*, 1979, p. 15). The thrust of global education is interdisciplinary; it is not another "add-on" subject but a way of perceiving the curriculum with a world view. It calls for the infusion of a global perspective into all disciplines so that the student achieves an awareness of other cultures, nations, and languages, and how all these are interconnected and interdependent (Bragaw et al., 1981, p. 53). It spans all levels of the educational spectrum.[2]

---

[1]*Strength through Wisdom: A Critique of U.S. Capability*, 1979. Available from the American Council on the Teaching of Foreign Languages, 385 Warburton Avenue, Hastings-on-Hudson, NY 10706.

[2]See *Bibliography:* National Education Association Project: *Education in the 80s.* Helene Z. Loew, "Global Perspective and Second Language Study: An Action Plan."

Global education was the main theme of the 1981 Northeast Conference (Geno, 1981). One of its reports, entitled "Global Responsibility: The Role of the Foreign Language Teacher," presents guidelines for *globalizing* the foreign language program (Bragaw et al., 1981, pp. 47-89).

In addition to cross-fertilization between social studies and foreign language curricula, various *exploratory* language-and-culture experiences from elementary through high school were advocated, such as the following:

- Teaching words and phrases in various languages to elementary school children in order to provide a "language-receptive mindset"
- Establishing exploratory courses in the middle school
- Incorporating an "introductory *linguistic* unit" into a beginning high school foreign language class. [Bragaw et al., 1981, pp. 68-70.]

The Exploratory Concept as Part of a Multidimensional Foreign Language Curriculum

The idea of a multidimensional foreign language curriculum was put forth in 1980 in Boston at the Conference on Professional Priorities organized by the American Council on the Teaching of Foreign Languages. The details of this conference have been reported in the *Northeast Conference Reports* of 1983 (Stern, 1983, pp. 120-46), as well as in the *Proceedings* of the conference, edited by Dale Lange and published by ACTFL.[3] The interested reader will find an in-depth treatment of the concept in the above-mentioned publications. A brief overview is given below.

The participants in the priorities conference[4] recommended a *multidimensional,* or multiple-focus, curriculum in contrast with current school curricula which are largely unidimensional and based on a situational-structural syllabus. They advocated four syllabuses integrated into one curriculum as a guiding concept for the future planning of foreign language course content: *linguistic, cultural, communicative,* and *general language education syllabus.* It is the latter which is directly related to the

---

[3]Dale L. Lange. *Proceedings of the National Conference on Professional Priorities, 1980.* American Council on the Teaching of Foreign Languages, 358 Warburton Ave., Hastings-on-Hudson, NY 10706.

[4]Participants in the ACTFL Conference on Professional Priorities (1980): Robert Lafayette, Lorraine Strasheim, Wilga Rivers, H. H. Stern, Albert Valdman, Robert Zais, and Helen Warner-Burke (Stern, 1983, p. 120).

content of exploratory courses as described in this text. The main themes of the general language education syllabus would include knowledge about language, culture, and society in general, leading to a general awareness of language and language learning (Stern, 1983, p. 132). Conference participants envisaged several possible configurations of a general language curriculum:

- As preparatory, preceding a second-language program
- As incidental observations accompanying the linguistic, cultural, and communicative syllabuses
- As a separate course associated with the foreign language program.

Similar recommendations were made by Hawkins in his recent text, *Modern Languages in the Curriculum* (1981, pp. 236-39; 292-306), in which he advocates "an awareness of language" course as a bridge linking the mother tongue with the foreign language. Although Hawkins advocated this course for British schools, the content he suggested closely resembles the linguistic component of many American exploratory courses, such as languages across the world, origin of languages, relationships, comparisons and contrasts, and the language learning process (Stern, 1983, p. 133).

The above developments, the continuing "grass roots" growth of the movement as reported in the literature (Omaggio, 1983, pp. 38, 39), and the results of the recent informal national survey conducted by the authors[5] indicate that the exploratory concept is alive and flourishing. Foreign language educators and school administrators are once again expressing the view that learning *about* language is an important part of foreign language acquisition. *Exploration* of language and cultures is again perceived as educationally enriching.

As perceptions are refined, awareness grows that future application of the concept need not be limited to a presequential configuration, since exploration may be experienced through one group of languages and cultures while the student is engaged in sequential study of another.

The 1983 Northeast Conference took the position that some form of foreign language study should be part of the basic core curriculum of all students at the secondary school level (Omaggio, 1983, p. 47). The exploratory concept may serve as an "organizing principle" to meet this need.

---

[5]Survey (1984) results reported in chapter 2.

Teacher Education—The Key to the Future of the Exploratory Concept

At present most of the training for teaching exploratory courses must be accomplished at the *in-service* level since teachers by and large have not had this type of training. However, if preparation for teaching exploratory courses remains solely in the in-service realm, the concept may be relegated to the tenuous category of a "frill" or extracurricular offering. On the other hand, elevating the preparation of teachers for exploratory courses to the *preservice* level affords the concept a status attributed by the profession to other preservice content courses. Such a move would demonstrate the serious commitment of the profession to the rationale and goals of the exploratory renaissance. It would also assure the sustained support of these courses in the secondary school curriculum.

The education of the prospective foreign language teacher, however, must have *breadth* as well as *depth* if the exploratory concept is to be established as a standard component of foreign language curricula of the future.

APPENDIX A—Part I

Survey for Curriculum Development

Exploratory Foreign Language Course
in Middle or Early Junior High School

I. Please indicate below the type of exploratory foreign language course offered in your middle or junior high school.

  A. ☐ *Language Potpourri*
  (Pupils are exposed to several languages for successive periods of time.)

  B. ☐ *General Language Course*
  (Course theme is study of language per se, relationship among various languages, etc.)

  C. ☐ A fusion of *A* and *B*.

  D. ☐ OTHER: Please describe briefly.

II. **CONCEPT INVENTORY**
    Below are three open-ended lists of unifying concepts or "universals" which might form a basis for developing curriculum for exploratory foreign language courses. The three categories addressed are *language, culture,* and *career awareness*.
    Check the square which reflects the level of emphasis given each concept in the design of the exploratory course offered in your school system.

  Note: Respondents are invited to *write in* other concepts they consider important. Indicate level of emphasis.

CODE:	H (heavy emphasis)	M (moderate emphasis)
	L (light emphasis)	N (no emphasis)

A. *Language Concepts (across Cultures)* (a partial inventory)

	H	M	L	N		H	M	L	N
communication concept					agreement				
concept of language					tense (temporality)				
development of language					gender				
language families/ geography					inflection				
					modification				

A. *Language Concepts (across Cultures)* (a partial inventory) (cont.)

	H	M	L	N		H	M	L	N
ancient languages					negation				
artificial languages					pluralization				
development of English					borrowing between languages				
concept of dialect differences					cognate formation				
concept of slang					derivation				
sounds and meaning					prefix				
sound systems					root				
"accent"					suffix				
stress					translation (limitations)				
melody					gestures				
animal sounds					signs/symbols				
words (concept of meaning)					writing/alphabets				
word order					dictionaries				
word forms					science/art of language study				
word form relationships									
word order relationships					OTHERS:				

B. *Cultural Concepts (across Cultures)* (a partial inventory)

	H	M	L	N		H	M	L	N
culture, meaning					famous figures				
culture contrasts					humor				
culture in language					greetings				
cultural connotation: words, phrases, gestures					names/titles				
language in culture					family				
proprieties and improprieties (across cultures)					friendship				
					roles of children				
					roles of men				
time across cultures					roles of women				
					homes				
education					religion				
schools (buildings and curriculum)					patriotism				
government/politics					foods: preparation/ dining				
facts of geography					self-concept across cultures				
facts of commerce									
facts of industry					awareness of researching a culture				
buildings									
performing arts					empathy				
sports					wariness of stereotyping				
holidays/festivals					ethnic heritage—U.S.A.				
myths/legends					OTHERS:				

C. *Career Awareness Concepts* (a partial inventory)

	H	M	L	N
concept of work (paid/nonpaid)				
career/occupation				
leisure				
occupational clustering				
interdependence of all workers				
interrelationship of all work				
why people work				
value of simulation				
self-identity/ self-appraisal				
work choice and personality				
occupational choice				
work standards and school				

	H	M	L	N
work values and standards				
school subjects/work world				
foreign languages/work world				
"hands-on" concept				
work across cultures				
work values across cultures				
work roles across cultures (including ancient cultures)				
world of work across cultures				
measurement across cultures (metric system)				
OTHERS:				

III. Kindly list the main *system goals* of your course.

IV. Please list the main *student performance objectives* for the course.

Appendix A—Part 2
Survey Results

The number of educational institutions queried was 111. Of the 48 respondents, 10 reported that their program was of the FLES type rather than exploratory. Hence, they are not included in this summary. Trends among the 38 reporting an exploratory course are presented in Tables 1-4.

The summary of Parts III and IV of the survey (system goals and student objectives) is presented in Figures 4-1 and 4-2 of chapter 4.

Table 1: Type of exploratory courses among 38 school system respondents to curriculum survey

Course Type	Number
Language potpourri	12
General language	4
Combination of above	14
Other	8
Total	38

Table 2: Levels of emphasis assigned to language concepts by survey respondents
(Expressed in percentage of respondents)

(N = 38)

Language Concepts	H	% M	L	N
communication concept	87	5	5	3
words (concept of meaning)	55	32	8	5
concept of language	53	31	16	0
sounds and meaning	53	31	10	5
sound system	42	39	18	0
"accent"	24	53	21	3
borrowing between languages	38	38	21	5
cognate formation	45	24	26	5
gender	29	39	24	8
gestures	38	29	29	5
writing/alphabets	24	45	31	0
inflection	29	34	31	5
word order	34	29	34	3
language families/geography	16	47	34	3
word forms	26	34	31	3
word form relationships	18	42	29	10
word order relationships	18	42	29	10
agreement	21	38	34	8
signs/symbols	16	42	38	5
derivation	24	31	47	16
stress	29	26	29	16
negation	24	29	31	16
pluralization	18	34	29	18
melody	18	34	21	21
development of English	10	39	31	18
development of language	10	38	45	8
tense (temporality)	18	24	38	21
roots	13	29	45	13
science/art of language study	10	31	26	31
prefix	10	31	39	18
suffix	10	29	34	26
translation (limitations)	5	31	47	16

modification	29	34	31	5
dictionaries	13	16	53	18
concept of dialect differences	8	16	60	16
animal sounds	0	21	37	39
concept of slang	3	13	55	26
ancient languages	3	8	55	34
artificial languages	0	8	29	63

NOTE: Levels of emphasis: H (Heavy); M (Moderate); L (Light); N (None)
    Reference: Appendix A, Part 3.

Table 3: Levels of emphasis assigned to cultural concepts by survey respondents (Expressed in percentage of respondents)

(N = 38)

Cultural Concepts	H	% M	L	N
greetings	92	8	0	0
names/titles	89	5	5	0
proprieties and improprieties (across cultures)	38	55	16	3
language in culture	39	53	8	0
wariness of stereotyping	74	16	11	0
foods: preparation/dining	68	21	11	3
cultural connotation: words, phrases, gestures	45	42	10	3
culture contrasts	58	26	13	3
friendship	50	34	16	0
culture in language	55	29	13	3
culture, meaning	55	26	16	3
family	74	5	5	0
homes	50	29	21	0
ethnic heritage—U.S.A.	47	29	21	3
empathy	32	42	21	5
holidays/festivals	34	37	26	3

famous figures	5	63	26	5
roles of women	16	50	47	0
sports	8	53	37	3
roles of children	18	45	37	0
roles of men	18	45	37	0
time across cultures	16	39	26	18
education	16	39	39	5
humor	8	47	39	0
facts of geography	16	39	45	0
self-concept across cultures	8	45	37	11
schools (buildings and curriculum)	5	47	42	5
myths/legends	5	45	45	5
religion	5	42	53	0
patriotism	13	34	45	8
awareness of researching a culture	16	24	45	16
buildings	5	26	47	21
performing arts	5	24	55	16
government/politics	3	24	66	8
facts of commerce	5	16	60	18
facts of industry	3	16	63	18
appreciation	2	0	0	0
immigrants—contribution	2	0	0	0

NOTE: Levels of emphasis: H (Heavy); M (Moderate); L (Light); N (None)
      Reference: Appendix A, Part 3.

Table 4: Levels of emphasis assigned to career awareness concepts by survey respondents (Expressed in percentage of respondents)

(N = 38)

Career Awareness Concepts	%			
	H	M	L	N
foreign languages/work world	21	50	13	16
leisure	10	53	31	5

career/occupation	16	39	32	13
school subjects/work world	24	26	34	16
self-identity/self-appraisal	24	21	34	21
work across cultures	5	39	34	21
work values across cultures	8	34	29	29
work standards and school	8	34	42	16
work roles across cultures (including ancient cultures)	10	31	29	29
measurement across cultures (metric system)	8	32	45	16
world of work across cultures	18	21	29	31
work values and standards	8	31	31	24
concept of work (paid/nonpaid)	8	29	39	24
work choice and personality	8	24	34	34
occupational choice	10	21	39	29
"hands-on" concept	24	16	24	37
value of simulation	0	26	24	50
why people work	13	13	26	47
occupational clustering	5	18	45	32
interrelationship of all work	3	16	24	57
interdependence of all workers	0	3	26	60
self-concept	2	0	0	0

NOTE: Levels of Emphasis: H (Heavy); M (Moderate); L (Light); N (None).
    Reference: Appendix A, Part 3.

Appendix A—Part 3

Concept Inventory—Levels of Emphasis—Total Responses

CODE:	H (heavy emphasis)	M (moderate emphasis)
	L (light emphasis)	N (no emphasis)

Results of *Survey for Curriculum Development.* Number of schools or systems responding: *38.* Although the total number responding to *Survey* was *48,* ten of these described FLES programs which are not germane to this study.

A. *Language Concepts (across Cultures)* (a partial inventory)*

	H	M	L	N
communication concept	33	2	2	1
concept of language	20	12	6	0
development of language	4	14	17	3
language families/ geography	6	18	13	1
ancient languages	1	3	21	13
artificial languages	0	3	11	24
development of English	4	15	12	7
concept of dialect differences	3	6	23	6
concept of slang	1	5	21	10
sounds and meaning	20	12	4	2
sound systems	16	15	7	0
"accent"	9	20	8	1
stress	11	10	11	6
melody	7	13	8	8
animal sounds	0	8	14	15
words (concept of meaning)	21	12	3	2
word order	13	11	13	1
word forms	10	13	12	3
word form relationships	7	16	11	4
word order relationships	7	16	11	4

	H	M	L	N
agreement	8	14	13	3
tense (temporality)	7	9	14	8
gender	11	15	9	3
inflection	11	13	12	2
modification	7	7	16	8
negation	9	11	12	6
pluralization	7	13	11	7
borrowing between languages	14	14	8	2
cognate formation	17	9	10	2
derivation	9	12	14	3
prefix	4	12	15	7
root	5	11	17	5
suffix	4	11	13	10
translation (limitations)	2	12	18	6
gestures	14	11	11	2
signs/symbols	6	16	14	2
writing/alphabets	9	17	12	0
dictionaries	5	6	20	7
science/art of language study	4	12	10	12
OTHERS:				

B. *Cultural Concepts (across Cultures)* (a partial inventory)*

	H	M	L	N
culture, meaning	21	10	6	1
culture contrasts	22	10	5	1
culture in language	21	11	5	1
cultural connotation: words, phrases, gestures	17	16	4	1
language in culture	15	20	3	0
proprieties and improprieties (across cultures)	14	17	6	1
time across cultures	6	15	10	7
education	6	15	15	2
schools (buildings and curriculum)	2	18	16	2

	H	M	L	N
government/politics	1	9	25	3
facts of geography	6	15	17	0
facts of commerce	2	6	23	7
facts of industry	1	6	24	7
buildings	2	10	18	8
performing arts	2	9	21	6
sports	3	20	14	1
holidays/festivals	13	14	10	1
myths/legends	2	17	17	2
famous figures	2	24	10	2
humor	3	18	15	0

*Note: Figure in each square equals number of respondents (school systems)

B. *Cultural Concepts (across Cultures)* (a partial inventory) (cont.)*

	H	M	L	N
greetings	35	3	0	0
names/titles	34	2	2	0
family	28	7	2	1
friendship	19	13	6	0
roles of children	7	17	14	0
roles of men	7	17	14	0
roles of women	6	19	18	0
homes	19	11	8	0
religion	2	16	20	0
patriotism	5	13	17	3
foods: preparation/ dining	25	8	4	1

	H	M	L	N
self-concept across cultures	3	17	14	4
awareness of researching a culture	6	9	17	6
empathy	12	16	8	2
wariness of stereotyping	28	6	4	0
ethnic heritage—U.S.A.	18	11	8	1
OTHERS: Appreciation	1			
immigrants— contribution	1			

C. *Career Awareness Concepts* (a partial inventory)*

	H	M	L	N
concept of work (paid/nonpaid)	3	11	15	9
career/occupation	6	15	12	5
leisure	4	20	12	2
occupational clustering	2	7	17	12
interdependence of all workers	0	5	10	23
interrelationship of all work	1	6	9	22
why people work	5	5	10	18
value of simulation	0	10	9	19
self-identity/ self-appraisal	9	8	13	8
work choice and personality	3	9	13	13
occupational choice	4	8	15	11
work standards and school	3	13	16	6

	H	M	L	N
work values and standards	3	12	12	11
school subjects/work world	9	10	13	6
foreign languages/work world	8	19	5	6
"hands-on" concept	9	6	9	14
work across cultures	2	15	13	8
work values across cultures	3	13	11	11
work roles across cultures (including ancient cultures)	4	12	11	11
world of work across cultures	7	8	11	12
measurement across cultures (metric system)	3	12	17	6
OTHERS: self-concept	1			

*Note: Figure in each square equals number of respondents (school systems)

APPENDIX B

Additional Examples of "General Language" Background Courses for Prospective Teachers of Foreign Language Exploratory Course

Included as possible models for teacher training institutions. (See chapter 5.)

Institution: Salisbury State College*
Salisbury, Maryland

Department: Foreign Language

Title: Language Differences: Educational, Economic, and Political Implications

Target Audience: Prospective foreign language teachers and teachers of English to speakers of other languages

Credit: Three credit hours (open to advanced undergraduates)

Format: Coordinated by the instructor; includes guest speakers on various dialects and world cultures

Institution: Frostburg State College*
Frostburg, Maryland

Department: Foreign Languages

Title: The French People; The Russian People; The German People; The Spanish People; also General Linguistics (Survey) [historical and sociolinguistics, as well as structural]

Target Audience: Cultural courses open to all students; linguistics course open to advanced undergraduates, foreign language and English majors

Credit: Three credit hours

Format: Taught by staff in the Foreign Language Department

Source of information: Telephone discussion with W. Palmer and J. Kerbow of Salisbury and Frostburg, respectively.

Institution:	Montclair State College**
	Montclair, New Jersey
Department:	Foreign Languages
Title:	Introduction to General Linguistics
Target Audience:	Required of foreign language majors; also as a general education course open to all students (fulfills Humanities requirement)
Credit:	Three semester hours
Format:	Taught by one instructor—focus on development of language, language structure, and linguistic and cultural relationships

NOTES:
In 1972 this course replaced "Foundations of Language" which had been offered for more than 25 years. The Foundations course had been the only course required of *all* undergraduates.

Related courses in English Department

1. *History of the English Language*—for majors, and as general education course, satisfies Humanities requirement.

2. *Classical Roots of English Vocabulary*—for majors, and as general education course, satisfies Humanities requirement.

Institution:	University of Wisconsin-Green Bay†
Department:	Senior Seminars Program
Title:	Seminars on interdisciplinary topics (cultural, linguistic, and sociological)
Target Audience:	Required of seniors for graduation regardless of major
Credits:	Three semester hours
Format:	Under aegis of separate department called Senior Seminars—interdisciplinary department drawing staff from all departments of the university.

**Source of information:* Milton S. Seegmiller, Chair, Linguistics Department, Fall, 1981.

†*Source of information:* Dr. Nikitas L. Petrakopoulos, Chair, Senior Seminar Programs, Fall, 1981.

NOTES:

Although one seminar is required for graduation, seniors may take more than one.

Pertinent Sample Titles

1. Language and How It Is Used

2. Language: Power and Style—(See course plan following this description.)

3. Comparative Perspectives on Race, Ethnicity, and Cultural Conflict in Modern Society

There are 35 seminar titles. Approximately 30 are offered each semester. This program was established in 1971.

A Senior Seminar

Professor C. Abbott
University of Wisconsin-Green Bay

Title: Language: Power and Style

In our thoughts and actions we both shape and are shaped by the language we use. Any people who share a language share an agreement on what the words and phrases of that language mean. That agreement is constantly being renegotiated. We are not often aware of the processes of that renegotiation and we are probably even less aware of how the agreements made affect our own thinking, imagination, and social contacts. But we cannot escape being affected.

This course will focus on that agreement. The course objectives are:

1. To understand better: how the agreement is negotiated; who or what exerts the most powerful influences; what we as individuals lose or gain in the process. Of special interest is the power we, as individuals or as members of groups, have in determining the kind of language we use.

2. To understand better what effects language has on our thoughts, attitudes, imaginations, perceptions, and social contacts.

3. To formulate and articulate individual attitudes toward language. Just as citizenship entails certain responsibilities and privileges so does being a speaker of a language. And just as there is a wide range of reasoned attitudes citizens may have toward the state, there is an equally wide range of attitudes speakers may have toward their language.

Plan of the course

The first part of the course will be devoted to meeting the first objective—to understand the power to shape language. We will do this through readings and discussions of four different perspectives.

1. The academic perspective of those who study the nature of language—in linguistics, anthropology, philosophy, logic, psychology, sociology, literature, biology. We will be asking what sorts of assumptions are made, what research programs are underway, what kinds of evidence they use, and what kinds of popularizations of their findings are reaching the general public.

2. The professional perspectives of those who use language for specific goals—advertisers, writers, doctors, lawyers, politicians, journalists, critics, bureaucrats, social activists, etc. Here we will ask what their purposes are, what kinds of assumptions they make, what is distinctive about their language use, and what kind of influence they have on the general public.

3. The perspectives of those who prescribe (or bemoan) our language use—English teachers, dictionary makers, columnists on language, etc. Here we would want to know what the bases of their prescriptions are, how successful they are in prescribing language use, and what would happen if no one paid any attention to them.

4. The perspectives of the day-to-day language of the people around us—regional dialects, slang, minority languages, social routines, etc.

The next section of the course will aim at the second objective: to understand the power of language to shape us. We can explore this through the following four areas.

1. The academic debate: does thought control language or does language control thought or both—from philosophy, psychology, linguistics, and anthropology.

2. The popularization process—what happens to ideas as they are transmitted through different language forms. For example, a study on coffee and cancer is published in the *New England Journal of Medicine*. The wire services pick it up and it is transformed into newspapers and the broadcast media. A few weeks later a reader writes to Ann Landers on the same information and she responds. What has happened to the information during these several stages?

3. Prejudice in language—how do prejudices (sexist, racist, etc.) get from people into the language? Can a language be purged of them?

4. Metaphors—some linguistic metaphors powerfully limit our thinking either because we fail to realize they are metaphors or because we have difficulty finding alternatives to the metaphors. Public policies are often built on prevailing metaphors. The metaphor of slums as cancers that destroy cities informs much of the government's attitude toward urban renewal. Is there an alternative?

Course requirements

Beyond attending class, participating in discussions, and doing the assigned readings, there are several required projects.

1. A question journal. Keeping track of the kinds of questions that occur to you can be a productive way of revealing your assumptions, attitudes, and interests. They are also helpful as guides toward more rewarding research topics. And they facilitate discussions of what makes some questions better than others. Students will all

keep such a journal to be turned in weekly to the instructor and to be shared periodically with the rest of the class. (Questions need not be answerable.)

2. A paper (the basis of an in-class presentation) on some influence on language. You may choose either to demonstrate how some person or group (preferably one close to your major area or experience) has had an effect on the general language, or to argue that some person or group should have a greater or lesser effect on language.

3. A paper (the basis of a second in-class presentation) on some influence of language on people. The options here are to demonstrate such an influence, evaluate an influence (real or potential), or to determine a program for counteracting an influence.

4. The final paper (in essence, the final exam) will be an opportunity for you to articulate your own attitude toward language. The format is to imagine you are responsible for writing a column on language for some periodical. You get to choose the periodical, and thus your audience. Your column should look at some aspect of language use and through it you should present the attitude you have formulated. Your column should also hazard some predictions about the future of the language and its speakers.

Readings

The main texts for the course will be the following two collections of essays:

The State of the Language, Michaels and Ricks, eds., 1980.
This book contains a collection of essays in each of the following sections:

"Proprieties"—right and wrong in language and who decides
"Identities"—how language marks group affiliation
"Media and the Arts"—jargons and other influences on language
"Ways and Means"—manipulation with language
"Societies"—language styles and their functions

Language in Public Life, Alatis and Tucker, eds., 1979.
Sections on "Public Language Policy"
"Language and the Professions"
"The Language of Public Persuasion"

The course will also make use of readings in the following works:

Keywords, R. Williams, 1976;
Language: The Loaded Wagon, D. Bolinger, 1980;
Sociobiology, E. O. Wilson, 1975 (ch. 8-10);
and a selection from the columnists:
John Simon, *Paradigms Lost.*
Edwin Newman, *Strictly Speaking; A Civil Tongue.*
William Safire, *On Language; Safire's Political Dictionary;* column in the *Sunday New York Times Magazine.*
Jim Quinn, *American Tongue in Cheek.*
Philip Howard, *Words Fail Me;* column in *The Times* in London.
Thomas Middleton, in the *Saturday Review.*

APPENDIX C

Exploring Computers and Their Languages

(Resource and Teaching Unit)

To the Teacher:

Study about computer languages can be a legitimate part of an integrated exploratory language experience, as is a brief exposure to artificial languages such as Esperanto.

The accompanying presentation, written for students, can be utilized in implementing the component of the exploratory course which deals with the development of *computer awareness* and of the concept that languages can be *invented* to serve a variety of purposes.

Teachers are urged to call on resource persons in the school and community to help provide an introductory experience and to become familiar with the computer or terminal before students are permitted to try it.* Students in a school which does not have a computer or a terminal might nevertheless gain some insight from the material in this unit.

In this document pupils are asked to find out the meaning of several computer language names. *Here is the key for the teacher.* (Pupils may find out by asking programmers they may know, checking with parents, math teacher, etc.)

> BASIC - given in this unit
> FORTRAN - *For*mula *Tran*slation
> COBOL - *Co*mmon *B*usiness-*O*riented *L*anguage
> APL - *A* *P*rogramming *L*anguage
> PASCAL - Named after French mathematician, *Blaise Pascal* (Pupils may investigate this famous French person as part of French Exploratory component.)
> LOGO - Type of computer learning system, including graphics, developed by Dr. Seymour Papert, Massachusetts Institute of Technology, Department of Research in Education. (Teacher may relate term LOGO to Greek word *logos* meaning *word* or *thought*—thus *logic*.)

LET'S EXPLORE COMPUTERS AND THEIR LANGUAGES

WHAT IS A COMPUTER?

The computer is an electronic machine that stores and uses information to solve problems. Another word for information is *data* (a Latin word that means "things that are given"). It is in the form of numbers, words, and various other kinds of symbols, and is typed into the computer on a keyboard. It is called *input*. It must be organized in exact and logical steps.

The word *computer* comes from two Latin words: *Cum* (with) and *putare* (to think); it has come to mean *to count*. A computer, then, is a machine that counts. The result of a computer's operations is called *output*.

Computers are divided into three categories:

To the Reader: A school may have a terminal connected to a central computer via telephone lines, or it may have one or several microcomputers.

Mainframe: This is a very large computer.

Minicomputer: This computer is smaller than the mainframe, but it is usually large enough to fill a wall. Remember the Latin prefix *mini?* Although *mini* means very small, minicomputers were so named because of comparison with the large-scale type. They are really not very small.

Microcomputer: The Greek prefix *Micro-* means *very, very small.* The microcomputer is about the size of a typewriter or small television set. It is the home or personal computer and can be used in the classroom.

Some high schools, universities, businesses, and research companies may have minicomputers; terminals can be connected to them by telephone. A terminal might have a screen which is the same as in a television set. It is called a *cathode ray tube* (CRT). Microcomputers also have a screen, or CRT. Some terminals print out the information on paper instead of on the screen. These are called print terminals. A printing device can be connected to terminals with a screen, or to microcomputers. This is called a *printer,* and it gives a printed copy of what appears on the screen. By the way, the screen is also called the *video.* Did you know that *video* is pure Latin, meaning "I see"?

Here is an example of a brief program written in BASIC.

(In BASIC, each line of the program must be numbered.* The computer must be instructed for even the smallest step. Remember, it does not think for itself!)

```
BASIC          100 DIM A$(25)
LANGUAGE       110 A$ = "sample string"
               120 PRINT A$
                   (The word PRINT tells the computer that it should print the mate-
                   rial that is represented by the symbol. In this case the symbol is
                   A$.)
               130 A$ = "new sample string"
               140 PRINT A$
               150 END
```

NOTE: Do not attempt to figure out the meaning of the example above. The purpose is to show what a simple program in the BASIC language looks like.

When the BASIC command RUN is typed, the computer will print the words *sample string* and *new sample string,* as it was instructed to do in lines 120, 130, and 140.

WHAT DOES THE COMPUTER DO?

The computer cannot decide what it will do, or what problem to solve. It cannot think. A person must give it instructions.

A person must be trained to tell a computer what to do. This process of giving the computer instructions is called *programming,* or *writing a program.* The person trained to work in this manner is a *programmer.* All programming for computers is called *software.* The computer and related equipment are called *hardware.*

---

*The numbering is usually done by 10's so that the programmer can insert other lines between the numbers. For example, between 110 and 120 one can insert lines 111 through 119 if it becomes necessary to add information and instructions in the program.

These instructions are recorded on magnetic tapes and/or discs. They are formulated in codes that have been invented especially for computers. The computer can carry out mathematical operations as well as other tasks. Its electronic circuits (contained in chips of silicon) reduce everything to counting in the *binary system*—in other words, *0* and *1, off* and *on*. This electrical impulse—*off, on*—is called a *bit*. Bit is a word made from *binary digit*. Eight bits equal a *byte*, which is the computer's "word." The computer's inner capacity to store information is measured by *Kilobytes*, usually abbreviated *K-bytes*. Remember *Kilo* meaning 1,000?

COUNTING SYSTEMS

In most cases, human beings use a counting system based on tens, or a *decimal* system. (*Decimal—decem* is the Latin for *10*.) Today's computers were designed to use the *binary* system, as we have already mentioned. In this system *two* is the base instead of ten. (*Bi-* is a Latin prefix meaning *two*.) Your mathematics teacher may help you discuss the *binary* system versus the *decimal* system.

    Example: The number *14* in decimal system form is *4* ones, and *1* ten.
           In the *binary* system it would be *1110.*

2	X 2	X 2	X 2	
Sixteens	**Eights**	**Fours**	**Twos**	**Ones**
	1	1	1	0

BINARY SYSTEM

$$\left.\begin{array}{l} 0 \text{ ones} \\ 1 \text{ twos} \\ 1 \text{ fours} \\ 1 \text{ eights} \end{array}\right\} \quad \textit{14} \text{ in binary (1110)}$$

read up

NOTE: In the *binary* system each position to the left of the previous position is multiplied by *2*. (You know that in the *decimal* system each position as you move to the left is multiplied by *10*.)

Other number systems can be invented, such as the one based on *twelves* which comes down to us in our clocks and other instruments for telling time. You may wish to investigate the origins of that system. This is called the *duodecimal* system. Why?

WHAT ARE COMPUTER CODES OR LANGUAGES?

The programmer provides the instructions to the computer in certain human codes which the computer reduces to the *binary number system* inside its electronic circuits. These codes are called *computer languages*. Several have been invented: new ones are continually being devised, and the old ones are continually being modified. The best known computer languages are:

BASIC
FORTRAN
COBOL
APL
PASCAL
LOGO (A system for student learning through use of the computer)
BASIC stands for *Beginners' All-purpose Symbolic Instructional Code.*

Try to find out the meaning of the other language names listed.

As you are learning in your Exploratory class, all languages are organized within a certain system, whether they are "natural" languages, such as French or Spanish, or whether they have been invented. In programming a computer you should not use parts of different languages; you must stay within the one designated to be used with that computer. Like people, some computers "know" only one language; others "know" two or three. One might say that they are *bilingual* or *trilingual.* (Find the meanings and derivations of *bilingual* and *trilingual.*) The fact is that the large computers have more circuits and can be programmed to use more than one language. They have a larger *memory.* Even with these computers one must not "mix up" the languages when writing a program.

Most of the smaller computers use some form of BASIC. Some feature LOGO. (LOGO is not really a computer language but a system for learning.) The set of rules for using a computer language is called *syntax.* The word *syntax* refers to operating rules of "natural" languages too.

ACCESS

In order to access (get) a program which is in the computer, one must know the procedure and code required by that particular computer.

WORDS TO REMEMBER

---

access	data
BASIC	input
bilingual	output
binary/decimal	printer
bit	program
byte	terminal
computer	trilingual
CRT	video

Can you tell where these words came from and what they mean?

References for Students
and Teachers

Computer Literacy (software package) *Introduction to Microcomputers, 1980.*

McGraw-Hill
1221 Avenue of the Americas
New York, New York 10020
(For TRS-80; APPLE II, PET microcomputers)

Computer Literacy: A Hands-on Approach, 1983.

> Luehrmann & Peckham
> McGraw-Hill
> (For APPLE)

Computers: From Pebbles to Programs, 1980.

> Guidance Associates
> Science and Mankind
> Communication Park
> Box 2000
> Mt. Kisco, New York 10549

> Filmstrips/Cassettes (teacher use with students)

Meet the Computer, 1977.

> Dodd, Mead
> 79 Madison Avenue
> New York, New York 10016

Mind Storms, Dr. Seymour Papert, 1980.

> Basic Books
> 10 East 53rd St.
> New York, New York 10022

Spotlight on Computer Literacy, Ellen Richman, 1982.

> Random House (School Division)
> 400 Hahn Rd.
> Westminster, Maryland 21157.

Story of Computers, 1977.

> Camelot Publishing Company
> P.O. Box 1357
> Ormond Beach, Florida 32074

The BASIC Handbook, David A. Lien, 1981.

> Compusoft Publishing
> San Diego, California 92119

BIBLIOGRAPHY

Adams, Ella. "General Language in the High School" *School Review*, 1935, *43*, 664-67.

Adcock, Dwayne. "Foreign Languages in Emergent Adolescent Education," in Gilbert A. Jarvis, ed., *An Integrative Approach to Foreign Language Teaching: Choosing Among the Options.* Volume 8 of ACTFL Foreign Language Education Series. Lincolnwood, IL: National Textbook Company, 1976, pp. 314-322.

Alexander, Wiliam M., et al. *The Emergent Middle School.* New York: Holt, Reinhart and Winston, 1969.

Alexander, William M., and Williams, Emmett L. "Schools for the Middle School Years." *Educational Leadership*, 1965, *23*, 217-23.

Arndt, C. O., and Kirkpatrick, Robert. "Exploring Foreign Languages and Cultures." *Modern Language Journal*, 1941, *25*, 435-42.

Augmenting Reading Skills through Language Learning Transfer. Indianapolis: Public Schools, 1978.

Bagster-Collins; Tharp, J. B., et al. *Studies in Modern Language Teaching.* Volume XVII of Modern Foreign Language Study of Canadian Committee on Modern Languages. New York: The Macmillan Company, 1930.

Bailey, Larry J. *A Curriculum Model for Facilitating Career Development.* Carbondale, IL: Southern Illinois University Press, 1971.

Bailey, Larry J., and Stadt, Ronald. *Career Education: New Approaches to Human Development.* Carbondale, IL: Southern Illinois University Press, 1973.

Baltimore County (Maryland) Public Schools. *Meeting Another Culture through French* and *Meeting Another Culture through Spanish.* Towson, MD: Board of Education, Baltimore County, 1972 (Curriculum guides).

Baltimore County (Maryland) Public Schools, *Foreign Language Appreciation—Spanish* and *Foreign Language Appreciation—French.* Towson, MD: Board of Education, 1978 (Curriculum guides).

Banathy, Bela, and Lange, Dale. *A Design for Foreign Language Curriculum.* Lexington, MA: D. C. Heath, 1972.

Banning, Evelyn. "Exploratory Course Cuts Language Failures in Half at Barnstable (Massachusetts) High School." (Grades 7-12). *Clearing House*, 1942, *17*, 10.

Barnes, Donald E. "Your Middle School Must Have a Revised Program." *Educational Leadership*, 1973, *31*, 230-32.

Basic French and Spanish Gestures. Portland, ME: J. Weston Walch, 1976.

Beauchamp, George A. *Curriculum Theory.* Wilmette, IL: The Kagg Press, 1975.

Beaujour, Michel, and Ehrmann, Jacques. "A Semiotic Approach to Culture." *Foreign Language Annals,* 1967, *1,* 152-63.

Bent, Rudyard, and Unruh, Adolph. *Secondary School Curriculum.* Lexington, MA: D. C. Heath, 1969.

Berlitz Editions Staff. *French for Travelers; German for Travelers; Spanish for Travelers; Latin-American Spanish for Travelers.* Riverside, NJ: Crowell-Collier and Macmillan, Inc., 1970.

Beusch, Ann A., and De Lorenzo, William. "Blending Career Education Concepts with the Foreign Language Curriculum: Responding to the Challenge." *Foreign Language Annals,* 1977, *10,* 9-17.

Bigelow, Barbara. *A Course of Study in Introduction to Language.* Unpublished Classroom Guide, 1963 (Available from author—R. R. #1, Box 27-A; North Conway, NH 03860).

Blancké, Wilton W. "General Language as a Prognosis of Success in Foreign Language Study." *German Quarterly,* 1939, *12,* 71-80.

Blancké, Wilton W. *General Principles of Language.* Boston: D. C. Heath, 1953 (original 1935).

Bloom, Benjamin; Engelhart, Max D.; Krathwohl, David. *Taxonomy of Educational Objectives.* New York: David McKay Company, 1956. (Handbook I: Cognitive Domain; Handbook II: Affective Domain).

Born, Warren, ed. *Northeast Conference Reports—1975; Goals Clarification: Curriculum, Teaching, Evaluation.* Middlebury, VT: Northeast Conference on Teaching Foreign Languages, 1975.

Bough, Max E. "The Intermediate Schools: The Junior High and Middle Schools." *Contemporary Education,* 1973, *44,* 271-74.

Bourque, Jane, and Chehy, Linda. "Exploratory Language and Culture: A Unique Program." *Foreign Language Annals,* 1976, *9,* 10-16.

Bragaw, Donald; Loew, Helene; et al. "Global Responsibility: the Role of the Foreign Language Teacher." *Northeast Conference Report.* Middlebury, VT, 1981.

Brannon, R. Marshall, and Cox, David E. "Coping with Real Problems in the Secondary Schools," in Gilbert A. Jarvis, ed., *An Integrative Approach to Foreign Language Teaching: Choosing Among the Options.* Volume 8 of ACTFL Foreign Language Education Series. Lincolnwood, IL: National Textbook Company, 1976, pp. 164-70.

Brenman, Morris. "A Modern Modern Language Course." *Modern Language Journal,* 1942, *26,* 275-87.

Brooks, Nelson. *Culture and Language Instruction.* New York: Harcourt, Brace, Jovanovich, 1966. (Pamphlet)

Brooks, Nelson. "Teaching Culture in the Foreign Language Classroom." *Foreign Language Annals,* 1968, *1,* 204-17.

Brooks, Nelson. "The Analysis of Language and Familiar Cultures," in *The Cultural Revolution in Foreign Language Teaching,* Robert C. Lafayette, ed. Report of 1975 Central States Conference in Foreign Language Teaching. Lincolnwood, IL: National Textbook Company, 1975, pp. 19-31.

Brooks, Nelson. "Retrospect and Prospect." *Northeast Conference Reports,* 1976, *22,* p. 167.

Bugbee, Lucy M., et al. *An Exploratory Course in General Language.* Chicago: Benjamin H. Sanborn and Company, 1926.

Campbell, Donald T., and Stanley, Julian C. *Experimental and Quasi-Experimental Designs for Research.* Chicago: Rand McNally and Company, 1963.

Career Education: What It's All About. National Association of Secondary School Principals. *Bulletin,* 1973, *57.* (Entire issue on Career Education.)

Carothers, Gibson, and Lacey, James. *Slanguage—America's Second Language.* New York: Sterling Publishers, 1979.

Carroll, John. "Foreign Languages for Children." *The National Elementary Principal,* 1960, *39,* 12-15.

Carroll, John. "Research and Language Learning," in Robert G. Mead, ed., Northeast Conference Reports, *Language Teaching: Broader Contexts.* Middlebury, VT, 1966.

Chomsky, Noam. "Linguistic Theory," in Robert G. Mead, ed., Northeast Conference Reports, *Language Teaching: Broader Contexts.* Middlebury, VT, 1966.

Cline, E. C. "Some Problems Relating to Exploratory Courses." *School Review,* 1930, *38,* pages 206-10 (a).

Cline, E. C. *Your Language.* New York: D. Appleton and Company, 1930 (b).

Cline, E. C. "A Theory and a Foreign Language." *Modern Language Journal,* 1921, *5,* 435-43.

Cole, Robert D. "General Language Courses in the Junior High School." *Educational Outlook,* 1931, *4,* 223-39.

Cole, Robert D. "The Old and the New in Modern Language Teaching." *Junior/ Senior High School Clearing House*, 1932, *6*, 286-91.

Cole, Robert D. *Modern Foreign Languages and Their Teaching.* New York: D. Appleton-Century Company, Inc. 1937.

Coleman, Algernon. *The Teaching of Modern Foreign Languages in the United States.* (Vol. 12 of 17-Volume *Reports of the Modern Foreign Language Study)* "The Coleman Report." New York: The Macmillan Company, 1929.

Coleman, Algernon. "Trends in Modern Language Teaching." *Education*, 1937, *57*, 391-402.

Coutant, Victor. "General Language and the Latin Teacher." *Classical Journal*, 1943, *6*, 347-59.

Crosby, Muriel. *Curriculum Development for Elementary Schools in a Changing Society.* Boston: D. C. Heath, 1964.

Daley, Mary E. "Language 8 at North Syracuse High School." *Modern Language Journal*, 1953, *37*, 38-41.

Disick, Renee S. "Teaching toward Affective Goals in Foreign Languages." *Foreign Language Annals*, 1973, *7*, pp. 95-101.

Di Virgilio, James. "Reflections on Curriculum Needs for Middle Schools." *Education*, 1972, *92*, 78-79.

Eddy, Helen M. *Instruction in Foreign Languages.* National Survey of Education, Monograph #24. (Bulletin 1932, No. 17) Washington, D. C.: U.S. Department of Interior.

Eddy, Peter. "Present Status of Foreign Language Teaching: A Northeast Conference Survey." (Thomas Geno, ed.) Middlebury, VT: Northeast Conference Reports, 1980, pp. 13-59.

Enwall, Beverly; Fearing, Percy; Saunders, Helen. *Exploratory Foreign Language Programs.* Position paper—National Council of State Supervisors of Foreign Languages. New York: American Council on the Teaching of Foreign Languages, 1975. (Mimeographed.)

Ernest, Anna. "General Language." *High Points*, 1942, *24*, 19-28.

Evans, Rupert; Hoyt, Kenneth; Mangum, Garth L. *Career Education in the Middle/Junior High School.* Salt Lake City: Olympus Publishing Company, 1973.

Fearing, Percy, and Grittner, Frank. *Exploratory Foreign Language Programs in the Middle School.* New York: American Council on the Teaching of Foreign Languages, 1974. (Unpublished manuscript.)

Feinberg, Susan. "The Classroom's No Longer Prime Time." *Today's Education*, 1977, *66*, 78-79.

Field, Thomas, et al. "Introducing the World of Language: A Linguistic Basis for Language Study." *Modern Language Journal*, 1984, 68, 222-29.

Finocchiaro, Mary, and Davis, Benjamin. "Contributions of General Language to a Changing Curriculum." *High Points*, 1952, *34*, 19-29.

Firth, Gerald R., and Kimpston, Richard D. *The Curricular Continuum in Perspective*. Itasca, IL: F. E. Peacock Publishers, Inc., 1973.

Florian, David J. *The Phenomenon of Language*. Wellesley Hills, MA: Independent School Press, 1979.

Forsheit, Samuel. "Why Aren't Foreign Languages in the Core Curriculum?" *Modern Language Journal*, 1954, *38*, 354-57.

Forum, vol. 3, no. 1. Association of American Colleges, 1818 R St., N.W., Washington, DC 20009. October, 1980, 1:7.

Foshay, Arthur. "Curriculum for the 70's." *An Agenda for Action*. Washington, DC: National Education Association, 1970.

Fouts, Clark M. "Trends in the Junior High School." National Association of Secondary School Principals. *Bulletin*, 1954, *38*, 9-21.

Friesen, David. "Middle School: An Institution in Search of an Identity." *Education in Canada*, 1974, 5-9.

Fryer, Bruce. "Free to Explore: Curricular Developments," in Gilbert A. Jarvis, ed., *Perspective: A New Freedom*. Volume 7 of ACTFL Foreign Language Education Series. Lincolnwood, IL: National Textbook Company, 1975, pp. 26-29.

Funk, Wilfred. *Word Origins and Their Romantic Stories*. New York: Bell Publishing Company, 1950.

Geno, Thomas, ed. "Foreign Language and International Studies—Toward Cooperation and Integration." *Northeast Conference Report*, Middlebury, VT, 1981.

Gordon, Jean, and Casey, John P. "Some General Ideas about General Language." *Ohio Schools*, 1953, *31*, 160-61.

Grittner, Frank M. "Foreign Languages and the Changing Curriculum." National Association of Secondary School Principals. *Bulletin*, 1974, *55*, 71-78.

Hawkins, Eric. *Modern Languages in the Curriculum*. New York: Cambridge University Press, 1981.

Hayden, Rose L. "A Beginning: Building Global Competence." *State Education Leader*, 2, 4 (Fall 1983): 1-3.

Heath, Douglas, "Affective Education." *School Review*, 1972, *80*, 1-23.

Higgs, Theodore V., ed. *Teaching for Proficiency, the Organizing Principle.* Volume 15 of ACTFL Foreign Language Education Series. Lincolnwood, IL: National Textbook Company, 1984.

Howard, James M., ed. "Competency Testing to Date." *Bulletin, Council for Basic Education,* 1977, *22,* 9-10 (a).

Howard, James M. "The Tyranny of Courses." *Bulletin, Council for Basic Education,* 1977, *22,* 14 (b).

Hoyt, Kenneth; Pinson, Nancy; et al. *Career Education and the Elementary School Teacher.* Salt Lake City: Olympus Publishing Company, 1973.

Hoyt, Kenneth; Rupert, Evans; et al. *Career Education: What It Is and How to Do It.* Salt Lake City: Olympus Publishing Company, 1974.

Hoyt, Kenneth. "Straight Talk on Career Education." *Today's Education.* (NEA Journal), 1975, *64,* 60-62.

Hutchinson, Mark E. "Languages in Post-War Education." *Modern Language Journal,* 1946, *30,* 256-64.

Irwin, Elizabeth, and Tharp, James B. "Developing the General Language Course." *Ohio Schools,* 1942, *20,* 6-7.

Jensen, Julie M. "Elementary Language Arts." *Education,* 1974, *95,* 61-64.

Johnson, Laura B. "Correlating through Cooperation." *Modern Language Journal,* 1939, *24,* 106-14.

Jones, Otho Eli. *A Study of Attitudes toward Career Education of Key Administrative-Supervisory Personnel in the State of Maryland.* Baltimore, MD: State Department of Education, 1974.

Karlin, Muriel Schoenbrun, ed. *The Career Education Workshop.* West Nyack, NY: Parker Publishing Company, 1978-1979.

Kaulfers, Walter V. "Observations on the Question of General Language." *School Review,* 1928, *36,* 275-83.

Kaulfers, Walter V. "Foreign Language Curriculum of the Future." *Hispania,* 1936, *19,* 13-24 (a).

Kaulfers, Walter V. "Magic Wand Solutions to Foreign Language Problems." *School Review,* 1936, *44,* 744-52 (b).

Kaulfers, Walter V. "Orientation Courses in Foreign Cultures." *Progressive Education,* 1937, *14,* 195-98.

Kaulfers, Walter V. "An Integrative Approach to the Social-Cultural Aspects of Language." *School Review,* 1938, *45,* 737-44.

Kaulfers, Walter V. *Modern Languages for Modern Schools.* New York: McGraw-Hill Book Company, 1942 (a).

Kaulfers, Walter V. *Foreign Languages and Cultures in American Education.* New York: McGraw-Hill Book Company, 1942 (b).

Keller, Howard H., and Ferguson, John W. "A Cultural Introduction to Foreign Languages." *Foreign Language Annals,* 1976, *9,* 50-55.

Kroll, Arthur, et al. *Career Development: Growth and Crisis.* New York: John Wiley and Sons, Inc., 1970.

Ladu, Tora. *Teaching for Cross-Cultural Understanding.* Raleigh, NC: State Department of Public Instruction, 1968.

Lafayette, Robert C. "Evaluating Cultural Learnings," in *The Cultural Revolution in Foreign Language Teaching,* Robert C. Lafayette, ed. Report of 1975 Central States Conference in Foreign Language Teaching. Lincolnwood, IL: National Textbook Company, 1975, 104-18.

Laird, Charlton. *The Miracle of Language.* Greenwich, CT: Fawcett Publications, 1953.

Laramore, Darryl. "The Classroom Teacher in Career Education." *NASSP Bulletin,* 1973, *57,* 93-103.

Lee, William R. "For and Against an Early Start." *Foreign Language Annals.* 1977, *10,* 263-70.

Leeper, Robert R., ed. *Middle Schools in the Making.* Washington, DC: Association for Supervision and Curriculum Development, 1974.

Levy, Sylvia N. "The General Language Course at Washington Irving High School." *Modern Language Journal,* 1956, *40,* 182-85.

Lindquist, Lilly. "A General Language Course as a Prerequisite to Foreign Language Study." *Modern Language Journal,* 1930, *14,* 285-89.

Lindquist, Lilly. "General Language in Junior and Senior High School." *Modern Language Journal,* 1937, *21,* 577-81.

Lindquist, Lilly. "General Language." *Modern Language Journal,* 1940, *24,* 563-67.

Lindquist, Lilly, "A Unit in General Language." *Modern Language Journal,* 1945, *29,* 9-17.

Lindquist, Lilly, and Wachner, Clarence. *General Language: English and Its Foreign Relations.* New York: Holt, Rinehart and Winston, 1968.

Love, William F., and Honig, Lucille J. *Options and Perspectives.* New York: Modern Language Association of America, 1973.

McGalliard, John C.; White, Dorrance S.; Lyte, Herbert O.; Joliat, Eugene; and Foerster, Norman. "A Statement in Answer to the Proposal to Substitute General Language for Specific Language Instruction in the Public High School." *Modern Language Journal,* 1941, *25,* 892-93.

Mangum, Garth; Becker, James W.; et al. *Career Education in the Academic Classroom.* Salt Lake City: Olympus Publishing Company, 1975.

Marland, Sidney P., Jr. *Career Education—A Proposal for Reform.* New York: McGraw-Hill Book Company, 1974.

Marland, Sidney P., Jr. "The Unfinished Business of Career Education." *Today's Education,* 1978, *67,* 57-62.

Masciantonio, Rudolph. *Word Power through Latin. A Curriculum Resource.* Philadelphia: Board of Education; School District of Philadelphia, 1973.

Mead, Margaret. "Early Adolescence in the United States." *National Association of Secondary School Principals Bulletin,* 1965, 5-10.

Michie, Sarah. "A New General Language Curriculum for the Eighth Grade." *Modern Language Journal,* 1938, *22,* 343-47.

"The Middle School." *The National Elementary Principal,* 1971, *51,* 8. (Entire issue)

Modern Language Association of America. *Values of Foreign Language Study.* Statement of Foreign Language Steering Committee in April 1956, in *Modern Language Journal,* 1956, *40,* 409.

Monroe County Community Schools. *Language and Man: Exploratory Program for Grade Six.* Bloomington, IN, 1972. (Mimeographed.)

Morain, Genelle. "Visual Literacy: Reading Signs and Designs in the Foreign Culture." *Foreign Language Annals,* 1976, *9,* 210-16.

Morgan, Bayard Quincy. "Language Study in the Junior High School." Editorial, *Modern Language Journal,* 1928, *12,* 658.

Morgan, Esther, and Williams, Emmett. "What Are Middle Schools For?" *Association for Childhood Education International,* 1970, 1-8.

Morrow, Judith C. "Exploratory Courses for the Middle and Junior High School," in *Student Motivation and the Foreign Language Teacher,* Frank Grittner, ed. Lincolnwood, IL: National Textbook Company, 1974, 119-43.

Müller, Siegfried. "General Language in College Curriculum." *Modern Language Journal,* 1944, *28,* 425-29.

National Association of Secondary School Principals. *Eighth Yearbook: The Junior High School,* Washington, DC, 1924.

National Association of Secondary School Principals. *Curriculum Report,* vol. 9, no. 5, Reston, VA 22091. May 1980.

National Study of Secondary School Evaluation. *Evaluative Criteria—Foreign Languages.* Washington, DC, 1960, *3,* 121-32; 1969, *4,* 117-28.

National Study of Secondary School Evaluation. *Junior High School/Middle School Evaluative Criteria—Subject Areas.* Washington, DC, 1970, 2, 61-71.

National Education Association. *Education in the 80s.* Cassette on Exploratory Foreign Language, with American Council on the Teaching of Foreign Languages, Washington, DC, 1982.

Nostrand, Howard L. "Empathy for a Second Culture: Motivation and Techniques," in Gilbert A. Jarvis, ed., *Responding to New Realities.* Volume 5 of ACTFL Foreign Language Education Series. Lincolnwood, IL: National Textbook Company, 1974, pp. 263-327.

Olinger, Henri. "Whither Foreign Languages?" *Modern Language Journal,* 1946, 30, 3-13.

Omaggio, Alice. "Foreign Language in the Secondary School: Reconciling the Dream with the Reality." Robert J. Mead, Jr., ed., *Northeast Conference Reports,* 1983.

On Campus. University of Maryland-Baltimore County. Vol. 3, no. 16, May 18, 1979.

Papalia, Anthony, and Zampagna, Joseph. "The Changing Curricula." *ACTFL Review of Foreign Language Education,* 1974, 6, 299-328.

Pax, Fr. Joseph. *A Look at Latin.* Oxford, OH: American Classical League, Miami University, 1969.

Pei, Mario. "Foreign Languages at the Crossroad." *French Review,* 1936, 9, 376-83.

Pei, Mario. *How to Learn Languages and Which Languages to Learn.* New York: Harper and Row, 1973 (Original 1966).

Poole, Jody. "Junior High and Middle School Programs: Exploratory Courses." *Bulletin,* Wisconsin Association of Foreign Language Teachers, 1975, 12-14.

Prince George's County (Maryland) Public Schools. *French for Travelers; Spanish for Travelers; German for Travelers.* Upper Marlboro, MD, 1974. (Curriculum guides.)

Prince George's County (Maryland) Public Schools. *Foreign Language Exploratory: Resource Guide and Handbook.* Upper Marlboro, MD, 1975. (Curriculum guide.)

Prince George's County (Maryland) Public Schools. *Foreign Languages—Middle School Guide,* 1980.

Prince George's County (Maryland) Public Schools. *Educational Master Plan.* Upper Marlboro, MD, 1975.

Pumerantz, Phillip, and Galano, Ralph. *Establishing Interdisciplinary Programs in the Middle Schools.* West Nyack, NY: Parker Publishing Company, 1972.

Rivers, Wilga. "Students, Teachers, and the Future." *Foreign Language Annals,* 1975, *8,* 22-32.

Rochester City School District. *Person to Person.* Linguistics Curriculum for Grade 7. Rochester, NY, 1975. (Curriculum guide.)

Rhodes, Nancy C., with Schreibstein, Audrey R. *Foreign Language in the Elementary School.* Washington, DC: Center for Applied Linguistics, 1983.

Roehm, Alfred. "Defending Modern Languages before Our Curriculum Revisers." *Modern Language Journal,* 1931, *16,* 228-31.

Sandow, Percy. "General Language—For Whom?" *High Points,* 1952, *34,* 20-21.

Seelye, H. Ned, ed. *A Handbook on Latin America for Teachers.* Springfield, IL: Department of Public Instruction, 1968.

Seelye, H. Ned. *Teaching Culture.* Lincolnwood, IL: National Textbook Company, 1975, 1983.

Sims, William D., and Hammond, Sandra B. *Award-Winning Foreign Language Programs.* Lincolnwood, IL: National Textbook Company, 1981, pp. 28-30.

Snedaker, Dorothy. "Pre-language Courses." *Modern Language Journal,* 1928, *12,* 295-98.

Steiner, Florence. "Career Education and Its Implications at the National Level." *Modern Language Journal,* 1974, *58,* 186-91.

Steiner, Florence. *Performing with Objectives.* Rowley, MA: Newbury House Publishers, 1975.

Stern, H. H. "Toward a Multi-dimensional Foreign Language Curriculum." *Northeast Conference Reports,* Robert J. Mead, Jr., ed., 1983, pp. 120-46.

Strasheim, Lorraine A., ed. *Foreign Languages in a New Apprenticeship for Living.* Bloomington, IN: Indiana University, Indiana Language Program, 1971.

Strasheim, Lorraine A. *This Stuff Is Hard! Outline of a Foreign Language "Readiness" Unit (Pre-textbook) to Help Students in Learning How to Learn a Foreign Language.* Bloomington, IN: Indiana University, Office of the Coordinator of School Foreign Languages, 1975.

Strasheim, Lorraine A. *Mini-Course Goals.* (Education F500/S520: Materials and Techniques for Developing Exploratory Foreign Language Programs—Summer program) Bloomington, IN: Indiana University, July 1976. (Mimeographed.)

Strasheim, Lorraine A. "German and Global Education: Why Study German in Indiana?" *Unterrichtspraxis,* 1982, *15,* 68-79.

Stratemeyer, Florence B.; Forkner, Hamden L.; et al. *Developing a Curriculum for Modern Living.* New York: Teachers College, Columbia University, 1963.

Stratford (Connecticut) Public Schools. *Curriculum Materials for Exploratory Course*, 1975. (Mimeographed.)

Taba, Hilda. *Curriculum Development—Theory and Practice.* New York: Harcourt, Brace, Jovanovich, 1962.

Taylor, Mark W., and Tharp, James B. "An Analysis and Evaluation of General Language: The Language Arts Survey Course." *Modern Language Journal*, 1937, *1*, 83-91.

Tharp, James B. "Can Foreign Languages 'Integrate'?" *Modern Language Journal*, 1936, *20*, 416-19.

Tharp, James B. "General Language—An Appreciation Course in the Study of Foreign languages." *Secondary Education*, 1939, *8*, 3-6.

Tharp, James B. "General Language Course and Its Administration." *Proceedings of the Ohio Workshop on Modern Language Teaching.* Ohio Council on Education. Columbus, OH: The Ohio State University, 1940, pp. 24-30.

Tharp, James B. "Future of Modern Language Teaching." *Modern Language Journal*, 1943, *27*, 460-69.

Topeka (Kansas) Public Schools. *Curriculum Materials—Foreign Languages Exploratory (FLEX)*, 1971-1974. (Mimeographed.)

Tursi, Joseph A., ed. *Foreign Languages and the "New" Student.* Middlebury, VT: Northeast Conference on Teaching Foreign Languages, 1970.

Valette, Rebecca. *Modern Language Testing.* New York: Harcourt, Brace, Jovanovich, 1967.

Valette, Rebecca M., and Disick, Renee S. *Modern Language Performance Objectives and Individualization.* New York: Harcourt, Brace, Jovanovich, 1972.

Vose, Dorothy F. "Foreign Language Exploration." *Modern Language Journal*, 1939, *24*, 22-27.

Waldman, Mark. "New Objectives in Modern Language Teaching." *Modern Language Journal*, 1931, *16*, 232-44.

Warriner, Helen P. "Foreign Language Interdisciplinary Programs and Activities." *Britannica Review of Foreign Language Education.* Chicago: Encyclopaedia Britannica, 1971, 125-61.

Wasley, Ruth E. "A Junior High School Exploratory Course in Modern Languages." *Modern Language Journal*, 1955, *39*, 187-90.

Wehr, Theresa, "A Course in General Language." *Classical Journal,* 1930, *36,* 194-206.

Ziegler, Carl. "The Language Teacher and the Amateur Language Student." *Student Motivation and the Foreign Language Teacher.* Frank Grittner, ed. Lincolnwood, IL: National Textbook Company, 1974, 107-18.

ACKNOWLEDGMENTS

The authors wish to acknowledge the help and support of their families in this endeavor. We are grateful for their enduring patience.

We also would like to express our appreciation to the following persons: Lorraine Strasheim, Indiana University (Bloomington) for having written the foreword to this text, and for her enthusiastic support of our work over the years; Irma Nicholson, our enduring and persevering typist.

To colleagues in the public schools of Prince George's County, Maryland: Patricia Barr-Harrison, for her dedication to the Exploratory concept, and for her contributions to this text; Virginia Hobble, who, as the first teacher of Exploratory classes in Prince George's County, beginning in 1973, has contributed significantly to the formulation of this curriculum; Dr. Louise Waynant and Dr. Monica Uhlhorn, who, as administrators, have facilitated the growth of this program.

To all other Prince George's County teachers who have helped to develop and to implement the Exploratory Course, we are especially grateful, most particularly to Gloria Curry, Linda Folk, Columbus Modlin, Roberta Dondes Stein, and Nadia Wasserman.

Finally, the authors wish to thank all administrators and teachers from school systems throughout the country who have so kindly responded to our surveys. We especially thank George Rundell, Topeka, Kansas, Public Schools; Art Micozzi, Baltimore County (MD) Public Schools; Jane Bourque, formerly Stratford, Connecticut, Public Schools; and Maria Wilmeth, Fairfax County (VA) Public Schools.

The responses and detailed information obtained from all the above sources have helped to shape the body of this text.

D.F.K. and W.E.D.

INDEX

NTC PROFESSIONAL MATERIALS

ACTFL Review

Published annually in conjunction with the American Council on the Teaching of Foreign Languages

Foreign Language Proficiency in the Classroom and Beyond, *ed. James*, Vol. 16 (1984)

Teaching for Proficiency, the Organizing Principle, *ed. Higgs*, Vol. 15 (1983)

Practical Applications of Research in Foreign Language Teaching, *ed. James*, Vol. 14 (1982)

Curriculum, Competence, and the Foreign Language Teacher, *ed. Higgs*, Vol. 13 (1981)

Action for the '80s: A Political, Professional, and Public Program for Foreign Language Education, *ed. Phillips*, Vol. 12 (1980)

The New Imperative: Expanding the Horizons of Foreign Language Education, *ed. Phillips*, Vol. 11 (1979)

Building on Experience—Building for Success, *ed. Phillips*, Vol. 10 (1978)

The Language Connection: From the Classroom to the World, *ed. Phillips*, Vol. 9 (1977)

An Integrative Approach to Foreign Language Teaching: Choosing Among the Options, *eds. Jarvis and Omaggio*, Vol. 8 (1976)

Perspective: A New Freedom, *ed. Jarvis*, Vol. 7 (1975)

The Challenge of Communication, *ed. Jarvis*, Vol. 6 (1974)

Foreign Language Education: A Reappraisal, *eds. Lange and James*, Vol. 4 (1972)

Foreign Language Education: An Overview, *ed. Birkmaier*, Vol. 1 (1969)

Professional Resources

Complete Guide to Exploratory Foreign Language Programs, *Kennedy and de Lorenzo*

Award-Winning Foreign Language Programs: Prescriptions for Success, *Sims and Hammond*

Living in Latin America: A Case Study in Cross-Cultural Communication, *Gorden*

Teaching Culture: Strategies for Intercultural Communication, *Seelye*

Individualized Foreign Language Instruction, *Grittner and LaLeike*

Oral Communication Testing, *Linder*

Transcription and Transliteration, *Wellisch*

ABC's of Languages and Linguistics

 For further information or a current catalog, write:
National Textbook Company
4255 West Touhy Avenue
Lincolnwood, Illinois 60646-1975 U.S.A.